OLIVIA MAE BRADLEY

THE POSITIVE KITCHEN

First edition printed in 2024 in the UK
ISBN: 978-19-15538-28-4
Written by: Olivia Mae Bradley
Edited by: Emily Readman
Photography by: Ellie Grace
(www.elliegracephotography.co.uk)
Designed by: Paul Cocker & Cara Snowden
Sales & Marketing: Emma Toogood
Printed and bound in the UK by
Bell & Bain Ltd, Glasgow

Published by Meze Publishing Limited
Unit 1b, 2 Kelham Square
Kelham Riverside
Sheffield S3 8SD
Web: www.mezepublishing.co.uk
Telephone: 0114 275 7709
Email: info@mezepublishing.co.uk

Contents

Breakfasts

5 Meals for 2 for Under £30

Lunches & Meal Prep

What's For Tea?

About Me

For those who might not have followed me on social media previously, I'm Liv, a content creator and now author (eek). I live in a little village in West Yorkshire with my cocker spaniel, Bennie.

I began my cooking journey in 2021 - thanks to lockdown - and it all started in my dad's little galley kitchen. It had a tiny window, and it wasn't very big, so at one point you couldn't move for all my stuff - I completely took it over with copious amounts of pots, pans, spices, and sauces! I began creating content in that kitchen, which ultimately led to me writing this book right now. I bet 2021 Liv never would've thought she'd be here three years later!

I've always been a foodie. I love eating out in new restaurants, ordering a cheeky takeaway, and hosting for my friends. As we were coming out of the final lockdown, I decided I wanted to try and build some healthier habits, and one of those was cooking from fresh and eating better, all while keeping it simple and fuss-free. I've always been someone who shouts from the rooftops about balance, especially when it comes to weight loss, and that's what I originally began to document across my social media platforms. I was losing weight in a healthy, non-restrictive, and sustainable way, and I wanted to share my recipes and my journey to help inspire others. In less than three months, I hit a 10k follower milestone and my @livthepositivefooodie journey truly began.

In the beginning, I experimented in the kitchen and tried to make my favourite takeaway dishes calorie deficit-friendly. I wanted to eat all the food I enjoyed while still losing weight. I ended up building the most incredible and supportive community from doing so, and as time went on, I used my social media like my own personal diary. I shared the ups and downs of my personal life and was dedicated to being transparent, raw, and honest in the hope it would help other people, too. Helping others is always at the heart of everything I do and share, and that's something I pride myself in when sharing content online.

Nowadays, I share a mixture of recipes, wellness, self-love, and lifestyle, and I'm showing people every day that you can build a life you love, no matter what setbacks and hardships you may face along the way. Food and positivity basically sum me up! I'm now doing social media as a full-time job, and I pinch myself over this nearly every day - never mind also being able to call myself a published author! I've worked so hard to get here, but there are no words to express just how grateful I am for the community I have online, and also for YOU, the reader. I just wouldn't be here without your support.

I've made this book with you in mind, so I hope you love it.

Crumb.

Acknowledgements

I want to begin by thanking **my incredible dad**. He is the biggest support in everything I do and, as I said at the start of this book, he put up with me taking over his house at the very beginning! He's a typical Yorkshireman: tight with his money but totally generous with the amount of unconditional love and support he's shown me all my life. I would not be where I am without you, Dad.

To Auntie Jo and Uncle Paul, thank you for letting me use your gorgeous home for the shoot. You are the biggest support to me, not just with the book but in every aspect of my life. And to **the rest of my family**, I am so blessed to have you all. I know **my lovely grandparents** would've been proud and I wish they were here to share this with me.

To my INCREDIBLE small circle of **amazing friends**. You've been by my side since the beginning, seen me through the lowest lows and the highest highs. I have absolutely won the lottery with you and my heart could burst with how grateful I am for you all. And yes, **Reece**, I've not forgotten about the holiday home in Barbados.

I would like to thank the absolute best thing in my life, my dog **Bennie**, but he can't read so I'll just give him an extra treat and hope he understands.

To the entire team at **Meze Publishing**, I couldn't have asked for a better publisher and team, and I'm forever in your debt for this incredible opportunity. To my fantastic and insanely talented photographer, **Ellie**, you are amazing, inside and out. You deserve all the recognition for bringing my food to life and making it look so good.

One of the biggest thank yous, obviously, goes to **my amazing followers!** Where do I even start?! Thank you doesn't seem enough. I must have done something right to have been blessed with the most amazing, kind, supportive community I could have ever asked for. I really would not be where I am right now if it wasn't for you guys, so this book is dedicated to you all. And to YOU reading this book. It means more than I can say.

The last and biggest thank you goes to **my incredible mum**. You supported me in every path I wanted to take in life, gave me the most incredible childhood, protected me, loved me unconditionally, and made me into who I am today. You have the kindest heart, and you show me the meaning of unwavering strength every day. Everything I do is for you. I love you and I hope I've made you proud. x

About the Book

Hello and a HUGE welcome to The Positive Kitchen! I am so happy you're here! This cookbook is full of fuss-free, budget-friendly recipes that are all 650 calories or fewer. It pretty much sums up the type of recipes I've been sharing online for the past three years, and I'm so excited for you to get stuck in and get cooking!

You'll notice that nearly all the recipes reuse the same store cupboard ingredients and they're all simple and quick. You won't need to go searching high and low for specific ingredients and you definitely don't need to be an experienced cook. These recipes are designed to be as easy and tasty as possible. Not only that, but every recipe is macro-counted too! They're all designed to be easily incorporated into your own health and fitness journeys.

Expect delicious grab-and-go breakfasts for those busy early mornings, no-reheat lunches for something fast and filling, meal preps to keep you balanced and on-budget, plus a chapter dedicated to my super-popular Budget Meal Plans that I've been sharing online! This includes four weeks' worth of meal plans (five meals a week for two people, all for under £30!), plus a shopping list for each week. All my recipes are cheap and cheerful, so make sure you stock up on the store cupboard staples beforehand! (See page 13). Finally, we have some delicious evening meals and fakeaways, including one of my all-time favourite recipes ever, my two-ingredient pizza dough!

The Positive Kitchen's aim is to make a positive impact on your daily life. It's here to help you save time and money, help you find a love for cooking from fresh, and show you that healthy eating doesn't need to be boring! Every recipe is made to be as accessible as possible and to leave your tastebuds feeling positively satisfied.

So, that's it from me! It's time to turn the page, get your cook on, and step into The Positive Kitchen. Enjoy!

Shopping Essentials

ALWAYS IN THE FRIDGE

Butter
Milk
Mayonnaise

OILS, SAUCES, AND VINEGARS

Olive oil
Sunflower oil
Sesame oil
Light soy sauce
Oyster sauce
Sweet chilli sauce
Tomato ketchup
BBQ sauce
Burger sauce
Sriracha mayonnaise (or sriracha hot sauce)
Apple cider vinegar
Rice wine vinegar
White wine vinegar
Balsamic vinegar
Worcestershire sauce
Lemon juice

CUPBOARD CLASSICS

Self-raising flour
Plain flour
Cornflour
Baking powder
Sugar
Honey
Vanilla essence
Beef, vegetable, and chicken stock cubes
Golden breadcrumbs
Sesame seeds

HERBS AND SPICES

Salt
Pepper
Dried oregano
Dried parsley
Dried basil
Dried coriander
Mixed Italian herbs
Paprika
Onion powder
Garlic powder/salt/granules
Ground cumin
Ground ginger
Ground coriander
Chilli flakes
Turmeric
Garam masala
Curry powder
Cayenne pepper
BBQ seasoning
Cajun seasoning
Fajita seasoning
Tandoori seasoning

Breakfasts

Start your day the right way! These breakfast ideas are some of my favourites to make. Some of these recipes can be prepped beforehand and easily reheated the next day, which is great if you've got an early start and don't have much time in the morning. If you're someone who struggles to decide what to make for brekky, hopefully this chapter will bring you some inspo!

Sourdough PESTO EGGS

PREP TIME: 5 MINUTES | COOKING TIME: 5 MINUTES | SERVES 1
CALORIES: 475 KCAL | CARBS: 49G | FAT: 21G | PROTEIN: 23G

This is one for my pesto fans! It's an easy but super delicious recipe and a great way to spice up your basic eggs on toast. You can also get it from pan to plate in about 10 minutes, so what's not to love?!

Ingredients

1 tbsp sunflower oil
2 tbsp basil pesto
2 large eggs
2 slices sourdough bread
20g reduced fat soft cheese
Pinch of salt and pepper, to taste
Chilli flakes, to taste

Method

Heat a tablespoon of oil in the base of a frying pan until very hot, then spread the pesto over the centre of the pan (where you'll crack the eggs).

Crack both eggs into the pan and cook for around 5 minutes. (If you want over-easy eggs, flip them about 35 to 45 seconds before serving.) Meanwhile, toast the sourdough and spread the soft cheese onto the toast.

When the eggs are done, pop them on top of toast and season with some salt, pepper and chilli flakes and serve immediately!

Breakfast BAGEL SLIDERS

PREP TIME: 15 MINUTES | COOKING TIME: 20 MINUTES | MAKES 6 PORTIONS
CALORIES: 340 KCAL | CARBS: 31G | FAT: 25G | PROTEIN: 30G

These breakfast bagel sliders are perfect for meal prep! They're freezable and taste just as good reheated. They're also really easy and cheap to make – what a winner! I use shop-bought sausage patties, but you can use sausage meat to make your own if you prefer.

Ingredients

1 tbsp sunflower oil
6 large eggs
6 sausage patties
6 bagel thins
6 single cheese slices

Method

Preheat the oven to 190°c, then take a large oven dish (big enough to fit 6 bagel thins) and lightly oil the base. Crack the eggs into the dish and whisk well with a fork. Transfer to the oven for around 15 to 20 minutes until the egg has cooked through.

Preheat the grill and add the sausage patties to a baking tray. Grill these for around 10 to 15 minutes. While the egg and sausage are cooking, slice your bagel thins in half, if required. When your egg has cooked, leave it to cool for a couple of minutes before using a spatula to carve out 6 equal-sized squares. Place a portion of egg on the base of each bagel thin.

Rinse out the oven dish, then place the base of the bagels in. Add the sausage patties on top of the egg, followed by a cheese slice and the top of the bagel. Return to the oven for 3 to 5 minutes to allow the cheese to melt.

Either serve immediately or leave the bagels to cool, wrap separately in tin foil, and freeze. If freezing, simply take one out the night before to defrost in the fridge and it'll be ready to reheat at breakfast!

Note:

To reheat the bagels, remove from the tin foil, place on a microwaveable plate, and reheat for about 2 to 2 and a half minutes until the bagel is piping hot throughout.

Cheesy Crumpet BREAKFAST BAKE

PREP TIME: 10 MINUTES | COOKING TIME: 25 MINUTES | SERVES 2
CALORIES: 542 KCAL | CARBS: 57G | FAT: 22G | PROTEIN: 26G

This might just become your new weekly brunch staple! You can use whatever breakfast toppings you fancy – the possibilities are endless.

Ingredients

2 tsp sunflower oil
4 sausages
4 crumpets, cut into halves
2 large eggs
50ml milk
Pinch of salt and pepper
200g baked beans
40g grated mozzarella
1 tsp dried or fresh parsley

Method

Preheat the oven to 200°c, then warm some oil in a pan and cook the sausages as per the packet instructions. Take an oven dish and lightly grease the base with oil, then add the halved crumpets.

In a jug, whisk the eggs, milk, salt and pepper together, then pour the egg mixture over the top of the crumpets, followed by the beans.

When the sausages have almost cooked, chop them into bite-sized pieces and scatter them over the crumpets along with the grated cheese.

Bake everything in the oven for 10 to 15 minutes until golden-brown and crispy, then garnish with parsley and serve.

Breakfast PIZZA

PREP TIME: 10 MINUTES | COOKING TIME: 15 MINUTES | SERVES 1
CALORIES: 520 KCAL | CARBS: 55G | FAT: 18G | PROTEIN: 40G

Yep, you're reading this right. You can eat pizza for breakfast without anyone giving you a funny look! Surprisingly, everything works super well together and it's a great way to enjoy something a bit different! Perfect for a tasty brunch.

Ingredients

60g self-raising flour
70g 0% authentic Greek yoghurt
2 tbsp tomato purée
Pinch of salt and pepper
1 tsp dried oregano
40g grated mozzarella
1 handful of cherry tomatoes, halved
2 bacon medallions, chopped into small chunks
1 egg
1 tsp fresh parsley, chopped

Method

Preheat the oven to 220°c. To make the pizza dough, start by mixing the flour and yoghurt in a bowl until it forms a crumbly texture. Use your hands to mould the dough into a large ball, then lightly flour a surface and roll the dough out flat.

Spread the tomato purée over the base and sprinkle over the salt, pepper and oregano. Top with the grated mozzarella, cherry tomatoes, and bacon, then crack the egg into the centre.

Transfer the pizza to the oven and bake for around 10 to 15 minutes until the cheese has melted, the dough is golden-brown, the bacon is cooked, and the egg is done to your preference. When cooked, garnish with some fresh parsley, slice, and enjoy!

Breakfast BURRITO

PREP TIME: 15 MINUTES | COOKING TIME: 15 MINUTES | SERVES 2
CALORIES: 467 KCAL | CARBS: 24G | FAT: 37G | PROTEIN: 34G

A delicious breakfast-style burrito! The fillings you could use are endless with this recipe, so feel free to add anything you fancy! These burritos can be frozen and reheated, so they're perfect if you want a quick, make-ahead breakfast for work the next day.

Ingredients

2 tsp sunflower oil
1 small red onion, diced
6 sausages, skin removed and chopped
2 tsp garlic paste
Pinch of salt and pepper
1 tsp paprika
1 handful of cherry tomatoes, halved
4 eggs
70ml milk
2 handfuls of spinach
2 tortilla wraps
60g cheddar cheese, grated

Method

Warm some oil in a pan and add the red onion, sausage and garlic. Season with salt, pepper and paprika and fry for 5 minutes until the sausage begins to cook through. Then, add the chopped cherry tomatoes and fry everything together with another pinch of salt and pepper. While the sausage meat is cooking, add the eggs and milk to a jug and microwave for 30 seconds. Stir, then microwave again for a further 30 seconds, repeating until you reach the desired scrambled consistency.

Just before the sausage mix has cooked, add the spinach and keep stirring until it wilts. Add the sausage and spinach mix to the centre of a wrap, then top with the scrambled egg and grated cheese. Wrap into a burrito and place back into the pan for 2 to 3 minutes each side until nicely toasted. Repeat with the second wrap. If freezing, allow to cool slightly before wrapping in tin foil and popping in the freezer.

Note:

To reheat the burritos from frozen, remove from the tin foil, place on a microwaveable plate, and reheat for about 2 to 2 and a half minutes until the burrito is piping hot throughout.

Hash Brown EGG MUFFINS

PREP TIME: 20 MINUTES | COOKING TIME: 30 MINUTES | MAKES 6
CALORIES PER MUFFIN: 205 KCAL | CARBS: 9G | FAT: 14G | PROTEIN: 16G

These egg muffins are great for an easy on-the-go breakfast! The hash brown base makes them deliciously crispy and they're a great high protein option, too.

Ingredients

6 frozen hash browns, thawed
Pinch of salt and pepper
6 bacon medallions
4 large eggs
60g cheddar cheese, grated
1 tsp fresh parsley, chopped

Method

Preheat the oven to 200°c, then take a muffin tray and lightly spray it with oil. When the hash browns have thawed, put them into a bowl with some salt and pepper and mix roughly to break up the hash browns. Take the hash brown mixture and mould it into each muffin cup, leaving a cavity in the centre. Pop them into the oven for 15 minutes until the hash brown mix begins to brown and cook through. Meanwhile, cook the bacon to your preference, chop it into small chunks, and set it aside. Add the eggs and grated cheese to a jug and whisk to form a smooth mixture.

When the hash brown cups have started to brown, take them out of the oven and pour in the egg mixture. Top with the bacon pieces then return the tray to the oven for a further 10 minutes until the egg has set and turned a nice golden-brown colour.

Finish with a sprinkle of fresh parsley and enjoy!

Chocolate Chip BANANA BREAD

PREP TIME: 15 MINUTES | COOKING TIME: 1 HOUR AND 5 MINUTES | MAKES 1 LOAF (6-8 SLICES)
CALORIES PER SLICE: 233 KCAL | CARBS: 36G | FAT: 4G | PROTEIN: 8G

I've always loved banana bread and this chocolate chip version is absolutely delicious! It's designed to be simple and easy – perfect for those slow Sunday mornings. It also makes the kitchen smell incredible!

Ingredients

150g plain flour
60g cocoa powder
1 tsp baking powder
½ tsp salt
3 medium bananas, very ripe
2 large eggs
2 tbsp caster sugar
50ml milk
1 tsp vanilla essence
50g chocolate chips

Method

Preheat the oven to 180°c and lightly grease a loaf tin. Combine the flour, cocoa powder, baking powder and salt and set aside. Then, in a large mixing bowl, add the bananas and mash with a fork. Add the eggs, sugar, milk, and vanilla essence and whisk everything together.

Add in half of the dry ingredients, stir until combined, then add the second half, making sure there are no lumps and the mixture is smooth. Stir in the chocolate chips, then pour the batter into the loaf tin.

Bake the banana bread for 55 to 65 minutes – it's ready when a knife poked into the centre comes out clean. Leave to cool on a wire rack before slicing into 6 to 8 portions!

High Protein
STUFFED FRENCH TOAST

PREP TIME: 10 MINUTES | COOKING TIME: 15 MINUTES | SERVES 2
CALORIES: 520 KCAL | CARBS: 62G | FAT: 10G | PROTEIN: 43G

A delicious weekend breakfast! This is a classic French toast recipe with a little twist… a delicious layer of vanilla Greek yoghurt in-between the toast! Not only does it make it taste amazing, but it's a great high protein breakfast option, too.

Ingredients

1 tbsp neutral oil
2 eggs
100ml milk of choice
2 tsp vanilla essence
4 slices bread
6 tbsp vanilla Greek yoghurt
2 tbsp golden syrup

Method

Add some oil to the base of a large frying pan and turn to a medium heat. In a small bowl, whisk the egg, milk and vanilla essence together. Take each slice of bread and dip it into the egg mixture, covering it well.

Then, lay the bread in a pan and fry on both sides – you may have to do this in a couple of batches.

Spread the Greek yoghurt over two slices of bread, then place the other slices of bread on top and fry on each side for a further 3 to 5 minutes until the bread is crispy.

Serve with a tablespoon of golden syrup drizzled over the top of each!

Lava Baked OATS

PREP TIME: 5 MINUTES | COOKING TIME: 15 MINUTES | SERVES 1
CALORIES: 442 KCAL | CARBS: 75G | FAT: 9G | PROTEIN: 24G

If you like baked oats, you will love this melt-in-the middle version! It's like cake for breakfast, and who's saying no to that?!

Ingredients

50g rolled oats
60ml semi-skimmed milk
1 tbsp cocoa powder
1 tbsp chocolate protein powder (optional)
1 banana
½ tsp baking powder
1 tsp vanilla essence
2-4 squares milk chocolate (or chocolate chips)

Method

Preheat the oven to 190°c and lightly oil a small ramekin.

Add all the ingredients (apart from the squares of chocolate) to a blender or food processor and blend until smooth.

Pour the oat mixture into the ramekin and push the squares of chocolate into the centre of the oats.

Transfer to the oven and bake for around 10 to 15 minutes until the oat mixture has set then serve!

Millionaires Breakfast OAT BARS

PREP TIME: 10 MINUTES | COOKING TIME: 20 MINUTES | MAKES 6 BARS
CALORIES PER BAR: 344 KCAL | CARBS: 54G | FAT: 9G | PROTEIN: 15G

Another great meal prep breakfast option! These oat bars are super easy to make as all the ingredients go into one oven dish. Add some protein powder to the mix to up the protein!

Ingredients

2 bananas
200g rolled oats
50g chocolate protein powder (optional)
½ tsp baking powder
2 tsp vanilla essence
200ml milk of choice
6 digestive biscuits
25g milk chocolate
4 tbsp caramel drizzle

Method

Preheat the oven to 180°c, then line a square ovenproof dish with baking paper and a few sprays of oil.

In a large mixing bowl, add the bananas and mash them with a fork, then add the oats, chocolate protein powder, baking powder, vanilla essence and milk. Mix everything together, then pour the mixture into the ovenproof dish and bake for around 20 minutes until cooked through and set.

While the mixture is cooking, smash up the biscuits in a small bowl. Add the chocolate to a small microwave-safe bowl and microwave in 10-second bursts, stirring and checking in-between to make sure it doesn't burn.

Remove the oats from the oven and sprinkle the crushed biscuit over the top, followed by the caramel drizzle and the melted chocolate. Leave to cool in the fridge for 30 minutes, then portion the oats into 6 equal-sized bars.

5 Meals for 2 for Under £30

This is the chapter I'm most excited for you to try! We all know the cost of living crisis is hitting people hard at the minute, and with the inflation of supermarket prices, a cheap food shop is a thing of the past. Don't worry, though! I've used my brain power to think of five delicious evening meals that'll serve two people for less than £30! The goal is to stock up on the store cupboard staples (see page 13), so you'll only need to go and purchase the "From the Shop" items. All my recipes use different variations of the same store cupboard ingredients, so you won't be buying anything you won't be using a few times! This keeps the cost of your weekly shop down so you're not over-spending on random ingredients you may not use again. I hope you love these meal plans and I hope they help you save a few £££.

Budget Meal Plan
WEEK ONE

5 MEALS FOR TWO FOR £30

SHOPPING LIST

From the Shop

300g thin cut beef frying steak or beef stir fry strips
650g chicken breast
Packet of halloumi
Ball of light mozzarella
0% authentic Greek yoghurt
Reduced fat soft cheese
Tzatziki
Red onions
Broccoli
Bunch of spring onions
Fresh coriander (optional garnish)
Half a dozen eggs
Tin of chopped tomatoes
Long grain or basmati rice
Spaghetti
Egg noodles
Garlic paste

From the Kitchens

Light butter
Olive oil
Sesame oil
Tomato ketchup
Sweet chilli sauce
Oyster sauce
Light soy sauce
Rice wine vinegar or white wine vinegar
Self-raising flour
Cornflour
Honey
Chicken stock cubes
Vegetable stock cubes
Sesame seeds
Salt
Pepper
Dried parsley
Mixed Italian herbs
Paprika
Garlic salt
Garlic granules
Ground ginger
Ground cumin
Ground coriander
Tandoori seasoning
Chilli flakes

Takeaway-Style TANDOORI TIKKA CURRY

PREP TIME: 15 MINUTES, PLUS 20 MINUTES MARINATING (OR OVERNIGHT) | COOKING TIME: 1 HOUR | SERVES 2
CALORIES: 501 KCAL | CARBS: 52G | FAT: 10G | PROTEIN: 47G

My go-to curry order is a classic tandoori chicken, and this version is a beauty! It's so easy to make. I always like to use a few drops of red food colouring to make the colour pop, too.

Ingredients

For the marinated chicken

2-3 large chicken breasts, diced
1 tbsp tandoori seasoning
1 tsp garlic paste
1 tsp ground ginger
1 tsp ground cumin
1 tbsp 0% authentic Greek yoghurt

For the curry sauce

1 tbsp olive oil
2 tsp garlic paste
1 red onion, diced
1 tsp ground ginger
1 tbsp tandoori seasoning
1 tsp ground coriander
1 x 400g tin of chopped tomatoes
Fresh coriander, to serve (optional)

Method

Add the marinade ingredients to a bowl with the chicken and mix to coat. Pop in the fridge to marinate for at least 20 minutes, but ideally overnight. When ready to cook, transfer the chicken to a baking tray and place under a preheated grill for 15 to 20 minutes until the chicken is cooked through and charred.

Meanwhile, in a frying pan, add a tablespoon of oil along with the garlic, onion, ginger, tandoori seasoning and coriander, then fry off until fragrant. Add the chopped tomatoes, then fill half the tin back up with water and pour into the pan. Leave on a low to medium simmer for around 25 minutes until the sauce reduces.

Add the cooked chicken and leave on a low to medium simmer for a further 10 minutes before serving with fresh coriander and rice.

Beef and BROCCOLI NOODLES

PREP TIME: 15 MINUTES | COOKING TIME: 15 MINUTES | SERVES 2
CALORIES: 576 KCAL | CARBS: 66G | FAT: 14G | PROTEIN: 47G

I love this one because it uses so many store cupboard staples, meaning it's super cheap and easy to make! It's a delicious and healthy alternative to your local takeaway, too. Winner, winner, beef noodles for dinner.

Ingredients

3 tbsp light soy sauce
1 tbsp white wine vinegar or rice wine vinegar
1 tbsp ketchup
1 tbsp oyster sauce
2 tbsp garlic paste
1 tsp ground ginger
3 egg noodle nests
1 head of broccoli, cut into florets
2 tsp sesame oil
1 beef frying steak, thinly sliced, or 300g beef stir fry strips
1 spring onion, chopped, to serve
Sesame seeds, to serve

Method

Make the noodle sauce by combining the soy sauce, vinegar, ketchup, oyster sauce, 1 tablespoon of garlic, and the ginger in a small bowl.

Meanwhile, cook the noodles as per the packet instructions. When the noodles are nearly cooked, add the broccoli to the same saucepan and cook them together until the broccoli has softened.

Heat the sesame oil in a wok or large frying pan, then add the remaining garlic. Fry the beef off until it's browned and cooked through.

To finish, add the cooked noodles, broccoli, and sauce, and stir together on the heat for a couple of minutes.

Garnish with some chopped spring onion and a sprinkle of sesame seeds!

Hot Honey HALLOUMI SPAGHETTI

PREP TIME: 10 MINUTES | COOKING TIME: 20 MINUTES | SERVES 2
CALORIES: 564 KCAL | CARBS: 74G | FAT: 16G | PROTEIN: 21G

Now this is one you need to try. Cheese and honey might be a classic combo but combined with pasta it's even more chuffing lovely! Just 30 minutes in the kitchen and you've got yourself a deliciously creamy pasta dish.

Ingredients

180g dried spaghetti
2 tsp olive oil
2 tsp garlic paste
80g halloumi, sliced
2 tbsp honey
1 tsp chilli flakes (adjust, if needed)
80ml vegetable stock
60g reduced fat soft cheese
1 tsp paprika
1 tsp mixed Italian herbs
Pinch of salt and pepper

Method

Begin by boiling the spaghetti in a pan as per the packet instructions. Make sure to reserve some of the pasta water to use for the sauce.

Meanwhile, in a separate pan, fry off the garlic in a little oil, then add the sliced halloumi and fry on each side until it begins to turn a nice golden-brown colour.

In a small bowl, combine the honey and chilli flakes before drizzling over the halloumi. Leave on a low to medium simmer to cook through.

When the halloumi is cooked, remove from the pan and set aside, but don't clean the pan as there should be some hot honey remaining!

Pour in the vegetable stock, followed by the soft cheese, and stir together. Season with paprika, mixed Italian herbs, and a pinch of salt and pepper.

Stir in the cooked spaghetti along with a ladle of pasta water. Add half the crispy halloumi, stir, then top with the remaining halloumi and serve!

GRANDESSA
Squeezy
HONEY

Halloumi and TZATZIKI FLATBREADS

PREP TIME: 15 MINUTES | COOKING TIME: 25 MINUTES | SERVES 2
CALORIES: 574 KCAL | CARBS: 70G | FAT: 20G | PROTEIN: 30G

A little taste of Greek! This recipe also uses the trusty two-ingredient dough method to make the most perfect, easy flatbreads. Topped with tzatziki and halloumi – you're in for a taste sensation!

Ingredients

150g self-raising flour
160g 0% authentic Greek yoghurt
1 tbsp butter
1 tbsp garlic paste
1 tsp dried parsley, plus extra to serve
4 tbsp tzatziki
80g halloumi
2 tsp olive oil
1 tsp paprika
2 tsp garlic salt
1 red onion, diced
40g light mozzarella (fresh, not grated)

Method

To make the flatbread, start by preheating the oven to 200°c. Then, mix the self-raising flour and the Greek yoghurt together until it forms a crumbly texture. Mould the dough into a ball with your hands, then divide it into two equal-sized dough balls.

Lightly flour a work surface, then roll the dough balls out to your desired flatbread shape, around 5mm thick. Combine the butter, garlic paste, and dried parsley, then spread it over the flatbreads. Place into the oven for around 10 minutes until the dough begins to cook. Take the flatbreads out of the oven, spread a tablespoon of tzatziki over each, and set aside.

Slice the halloumi into strips and add to a hot frying pan with the olive oil. Fry the halloumi on each side with the paprika and garlic salt. When they start to crisp, add them to the flatbread along with the diced red onion. Finally, tear up the mozzarella and sprinkle it across the flatbread with another sprinkle of garlic salt, and pop it back into the oven for 15 minutes until the cheese is bubbling and the dough is golden-brown.

Serve with another couple of tablespoons of the tzatziki, a sprinkle of parsley, and a crunchy salad!

Sticky Sweet CHILLI CHICKEN

PREP TIME: 10 MINUTES | COOKING TIME: 20 MINUTES | SERVES 2
CALORIES: 582 KCAL | CARBS: 77G | FAT: 12G | PROTEIN: 37G

If you fancy a midweek fakeaway, then you're in luck! This Sticky Sweet Chilli Chicken is a beautiful combination of flavours and only takes 30 minutes! Healthy, quick, and easy. What more could you ask for?

Ingredients

4 tbsp cornflour
1 tsp paprika
1 tbsp garlic granules
Pinch of salt and pepper
2 chicken breasts, cut into strips
1 egg, beaten
4 tbsp sweet chilli sauce
2 tbsp light soy sauce
2 tbsp rice wine vinegar or white wine vinegar
1 tbsp olive oil
1 tbsp garlic paste
1 tsp ground ginger
1 spring onion, chopped, to serve
Sesame seeds, to serve

Method

Add the cornflour, paprika, garlic granules, and a pinch of salt and pepper to a bowl. Dip the chicken breast strips into the beaten egg before dipping them into the cornflour mix, making sure they're fully coated. In another bowl, combine the sweet chilli sauce, light soy sauce and rice wine vinegar. Set aside.

Heat a little oil in a pan and add the garlic paste and ground ginger. Fry off a little before adding the chicken strips and frying until the chicken begins to brown and turn nice and crispy. Remove and set aside.

Add the bowl of sauce to the pan and heat for a couple of minutes until it begins to thicken. Turn off the heat, then add the chicken to the sauce and stir to coat. Serve immediately with rice, and garnish with spring onion and a sprinkle of sesame seeds!

LIGHT
SOY
SAUCE
간장
150ml

Budget Meal Plan
WEEK TWO

5 MEALS FOR TWO FOR £30

SHOPPING LIST

From the Shop

500g 5% fat beef mince
2 salmon fillets
2 large chicken breasts
Sliced pepperoni
Reduced fat soft cheese
Grated mozzarella
Grated parmesan
Red onions
Bulb of garlic
2kg bag of Maris Piper potatoes (optional)
2 bags of mixed bell peppers (6 peppers)
2 tins of chopped tomatoes
2 cartons of tomato passata
Tomato purée
Long grain rice
Lasagne sheets
Tortilla wraps

From the Kitchen

Olive oil
Honey
Light soy sauce
Lemon juice
Sesame seeds
Sugar
Vegetable stock cubes
Beef stock cubes
Salt
Pepper
Dried basil
Dried parsley
Dried oregano
Mixed Italian herbs
Paprika
Garlic salt
Fajita seasoning

One Pot LASAGNE

PREP TIME: 10 MINUTES | COOKING TIME: 40 MINUTES | SERVES 4
CALORIES: 413 KCAL | CARBS: 33G | FAT: 14G | PROTEIN: 36G

Not your typical lasagne, but one you'll want to keep making again and again! This one is made in a casserole dish and is so easy to do. Anything you can just throw into a pot is always a fave of mine (anything for less washing up, right?). This one makes 4 portions, so have some mates over or eat the leftovers up the next day for lunch!

Ingredients

1 tsp olive oil
2 cloves of garlic, minced
500g 5% fat beef mince
1 red onion, diced
2 tsp dried oregano
2 tsp dried basil
2 tsp dried parsley
2 tsp paprika
Pinch of salt and pepper
1 x 400g tin of chopped tomatoes
300ml water
1 beef stock cube
60g reduced fat soft cheese
8 lasagne sheets, broken into pieces
20g parmesan, grated
80g grated mozzarella

Method

Preheat the oven to 190°c. Add a little oil and the chopped garlic to the bottom of an ovenproof, hob-safe dish or pot and fry for a couple minutes. Add the beef mince and when it begins to brown, add the chopped onion and all the dried herbs, paprika, and a pinch of salt and pepper. Pour in the chopped tomatoes, followed by 300ml water. Crumble in the stock cube and leave the sauce on a low to medium simmer for 5 minutes.

Stir the soft cheese through until the sauce turns creamy. Add the broken lasagne sheets, making sure they are covered by the sauce, then sprinkle over the grated parmesan.

Transfer to the oven and bake for 10 to 15 minutes until the lasagne sheets are nearly cooked through. Remove from the oven, sprinkle over the grated mozzarella, then bake for a further 5 to 10 minutes until the cheese is golden and bubbling. Serve immediately!

Tortilla Pizzas and POTATO WEDGES

PREP TIME: 10 MINUTES | COOKING TIME: 40 MINUTES | SERVES 2
CALORIES: 380 KCAL (EXCLUDING WEDGES) | CARBS: 44G | FAT: 17G | PROTEIN: 16G

The simplest yet most delicious meal! Tortilla pizzas are often overlooked as a quick but filling dinner idea. You can load them up with whatever toppings you want, you don't need to make a dough, plus they're health and budget friendly!

Ingredients

For the potato wedges (optional)

3 Maris Piper potatoes, cut into wedges
Pinch of salt and pepper
1 tsp garlic salt
1 tsp paprika
1 tsp olive oil

For the tortilla pizza

1 tbsp tomato purée
2 tbsp tomato passata
2 tsp dried oregano
2 tsp dried basil
1 tsp garlic salt
2 tortilla wraps
60g grated mozzarella
8 slices pepperoni
½ red onion, diced
1 red bell pepper, sliced

Method

Preheat the oven to 200°c. Add the potato wedges to a large mixing bowl, then season them with the salt, pepper, garlic salt, paprika and olive oil. Mix to coat before transferring to the oven to cook for 35 minutes until golden-brown. If using an air fryer, cook for 25 minutes at 200°c.

While the chips are cooking, combine the tomato purée, passata, oregano, basil and garlic salt together in a small bowl to make a pizza sauce. Spread the sauce over two tortilla bases, then top the pizza with the grated mozzarella, pepperoni, onion and pepper.

Around 10 minutes before the wedges are cooked, transfer the pizzas to the oven and bake for 7 to 10 minutes until the cheese is golden-brown and bubbling and the edges of the tortilla have crisped up.Serve the pizzas with the wedges and your choice of sauce.

Fajita Chicken Enchiladas and POTATO WEDGES

PREP TIME: 10 MINUTES | COOKING TIME: 40 MINUTES | SERVES 2
CALORIES: 625 KCAL (EXCLUDING THE WEDGES) | CARBS: 74G | FAT: 18G | PROTEIN: 41G

A quick and easy comforting dinner that's so easy to make! I personally LOVE enchiladas and I feel like they're one of those meals that easily become a staple on your meal plan because they taste SO good.

Ingredients

For the potato wedges

3 Maris Piper potatoes, cut into wedges
Pinch of salt and pepper
1 tsp paprika
1 tsp garlic salt
1 tsp olive oil

For the enchiladas

2 tsp olive oil
2 cloves of garlic, minced
1 red onion, diced
1 red bell pepper, sliced
1 yellow bell pepper, sliced
2 large chicken breasts, diced
1 tbsp fajita seasoning
Pinch of salt and pepper
3 tsp paprika
100ml chicken stock
500g tomato passata
2 tsp garlic salt
1 tsp dried oregano
4 tortilla wraps
60g grated mozzarella

Method

Preheat the oven to 200°c. Add the wedges to a large mixing bowl and season them with the salt, pepper, garlic salt, paprika and oil. Stir to coat then transfer to the oven to cook for 35 minutes until golden-brown. If using an air fryer, cook for 25 minutes at 200°c.

Add the garlic to a pan with a little oil and fry for a couple minutes before adding the chopped onion and peppers. Fry until softened then add the chicken breast and season with fajita seasoning, salt, pepper and 2 teaspoons of paprika. When the chicken has browned, add the chicken stock and half the passata. Turn down to a simmer and allow to reduce.

In a separate small pan, make the enchilada sauce by combining the remainder of the tomato passata, garlic salt, oregano, salt, pepper, and 1 teaspoon of paprika. Stir on a low heat to warm through.

When the chicken and pepper mix has cooked through, divide it between the four tortilla wraps and roll them into burrito shapes.

Transfer the wraps to an oven dish, then pour the enchilada sauce down the middle of the wraps before topping them with grated mozzarella. Bake in the oven for about 20 minutes until the cheese is golden-brown and bubbling.

Pepperoni PASTA BAKE

PREP TIME: 10 MINUTES | COOKING TIME: 30 MINUTES | SERVES 2
CALORIES: 520 KCAL | CARBS: 82G | FAT: 16G | PROTEIN: 28G

Pasta bakes are the ultimate comfort food, and this one is sure to be a hit with the whole family! It's easy to make and super cheesy.

Ingredients

180g dried penne pasta
1 tsp olive oil
4 cloves of garlic, minced
1 yellow bell pepper, sliced
1 green bell pepper, sliced
1 red bell pepper, sliced
1 red onion, diced
1 tbsp tomato purée
Pinch of salt and pepper
2 tsp paprika
1 tsp sugar
1 tbsp mixed Italian herbs
1 x 400g tin of chopped tomatoes
1 vegetable stock cube
70g grated mozzarella
8 slices pepperoni

Method

Preheat the oven to 210°c then cook the pasta as per the packet instructions. Drain and set aside.

Add the oil and garlic to the base of an ovenproof casserole dish. Fry for a few minutes until fragrant, then add the sliced bell peppers, onion and tomato purée. Season with salt, pepper, paprika, sugar and mixed Italian herbs.

Pour in the tin of chopped tomatoes and crumble the vegetable stock cube over the top, stirring everything through. Fill the tin of chopped tomatoes halfway with water and add it to the sauce. Leave on a low to medium simmer for about 10 minutes to allow the sauce to cook through and thicken.

Add the cooked pasta to the sauce, stir through, then top with the grated mozzarella and sliced pepperoni. Transfer the dish to an oven, uncovered, for 5 to 10 minutes until the cheese is golden-brown and bubbling!

Honey Garlic Glazed SALMON AND RICE

PREP TIME: 5 MINUTES | COOKING TIME: 15 MINUTES | SERVES 2
CALORIES: 390 KCAL | CARBS: 25G | FAT: 17G | PROTEIN: 28G

This easy dish is made in just 20 minutes, instantly making it one of my favourite speedy weeknight staples. The sticky, garlicky sauce is SO good with the salmon.

Ingredients

200g long grain rice
1 tbsp light soy sauce
2 tbsp lemon juice
2 tbsp honey
1 tbsp water
1 tsp paprika
1 tbsp olive oil
4 cloves of garlic, minced
2 salmon fillets
Pinch of salt and pepper
1 tsp sesame seeds

Method

Begin by cooking the rice as per the packet instructions. In a small bowl, whisk together the soy sauce, lemon juice, honey, water and paprika until smooth.

Pop the oil and garlic into a pan on a medium-high heat. Add the salmon fillets to the pan, skin side down, and season with salt and pepper. After 5 minutes, flip and fry on the other side until the salmon begins to turn a nice golden-brown. Pour the sauce over the salmon and let it cook in the glaze for a further 5 minutes. Take it off the heat and serve over the cooked rice, removing the salmon skin if preferred. If there's any glaze left in the pan, pour this over the salmon and rice. Garnish with sesame seeds!

GRANDESSA
Squeezy
HONEY

CUCINA
MADE IN ITALY
PESTO
SUN-DRIED TOMATO

Budget Meal Plan
WEEK THREE

5 MEALS FOR TWO FOR £30

SHOPPING LIST

From the Shop

500g 5% fat beef mince
12 chipolata sausages
650g chicken breast (medium pack)
1 tub of double cream
Grated parmesan
White onions
2 bulbs of garlic
Carrots
Broccoli
Salad potatoes
Tin of kidney beans
Tin of chopped tomatoes
Tomato purée
1 jar of red pesto
Long grain rice

From the Kitchen

Light butter
Honey
Lemon juice
Balsamic vinegar
Beef stock cubes
Chicken stock cubes
Salt
Pepper
Dried basil
Dried coriander
Dried parsley
Dried oregano
Paprika
Onion powder
Garlic powder
Garlic salt
Ground cumin
Turmeric
Garam masala
Mild curry powder
Ground ginger
Cayenne pepper

Slow Cooker Chilli Con Carne AND RICE

PREP TIME: 5 MINUTES | COOKING TIME: 6-8 HOURS | SERVES 4
CALORIES: 490 KCAL | CARBS: 56G | FAT: 10G | PROTEIN: 46G

I love a slow cooker dish as there's nothing better than throwing everything in and forgetting about it until dinner! Plus, this recipe makes enough to have some tasty leftovers that you can enjoy the next day, which makes this classic dish one of my faves!

Ingredients

500g 5% fat beef mince
1 onion, diced
1 x 400g tin of kidney beans
1 x 400g tin of chopped tomatoes
2 tbsp tomato purée
1 beef stock cube
Pinch of salt and pepper
2 tsp dried oregano
4 tsp garlic powder
2 tsp ground cumin
2 tsp cayenne pepper
250g white rice, to serve (microwaveable, if preferred)

Method

Put all the ingredients, excluding the rice, into the slow cooker. Make sure to break up the mince using a wooden spoon. Cook on high for 6 hours or low for 8 hours. Serve with the white rice and enjoy.

Red Pesto Hassleback Chicken AND CRISPY POTATOES

PREP TIME: 10 MINUTES | COOKING TIME: 35 MINUTES | SERVES 2
CALORIES: 340 KCAL (EXCLUDING WEDGES) | CARBS: 3G | FAT: 15G | PROTEIN: 43G

There are so many variations of hassleback chicken, but I LOVE this red pesto and parmesan version – the flavours work so well together! Serve with some crispy potatoes and salad and you've got yourself a delicious evening meal!

Ingredients

For the crispy potatoes

200g salad potatoes
1 tbsp oil
Pinch of salt and pepper
3 tsp paprika
2 tsp garlic salt

For the hasselback chicken

4 tbsp red pesto
1 tsp onion powder
1 tsp garlic salt
2 tsp lemon juice
2 large chicken breasts
Pinch of salt and pepper
20g parmesan, grated

Method

Preheat the oven to 200°c. Add the potatoes to a mixing bowl with the oil, salt, pepper, paprika, and garlic salt and stir to coat. Transfer to the oven and bake for 30 to 35 minutes or, if using an air fryer, bake at 200°c for 20 minutes until the potatoes are golden-brown and crispy.

Meanwhile, combine the pesto, onion powder, garlic salt and lemon juice in a small bowl. Cut horizontal slits across the chicken breasts, around 1cm apart, then season with salt and pepper (be careful not to cut all the way through the meat). Divide the pesto mixture between each slit, then transfer the chicken to a baking tray.

Sprinkle the parmesan cheese and an optional pinch of paprika over both chicken breasts, then bake in the oven for 20 to 25 minutes until the chicken is cooked through and a nice golden-brown. Serve the chicken with the crispy potatoes and a side salad, if you like!

Sticky Pesto Sausage AND POTATO TRAYBAKE

PREP TIME: 15 MINUTES | COOKING TIME: 45 MINUTES | SERVES 2
CALORIES: 572 KCAL | CARBS: 28G | FAT: 32G | PROTEIN: 20G

The easier the recipe, the better it is, right?! This traybake is one of my faves because you can throw it all together and pop it straight into the oven, spending less time preparing and much more time enjoying. Feel free to add more of your favourite veg to the tray, such as tomatoes or onions!

Ingredients

1 tsp olive oil
8 chipolata sausages
1 onion, cut into wedges
2 carrots, sliced into rounds
1 head of broccoli, cut into florets
4 cloves of garlic, unpeeled
300g salad potatoes, chopped in half
4 tbsp red pesto
1 tbsp balsamic vinegar
2 tsp garlic salt
2 tbsp honey
Pinch of salt and pepper

Method

Preheat the oven to 200°c. Lightly oil a baking tray then scatter in the sausages, onion, carrots, broccoli, garlic cloves and potatoes. In a small dish, combine the red pesto, balsamic vinegar, garlic salt and honey. Drizzle this all over the baking tray, making sure the vegetables and sausages are evenly coated.

Transfer to the oven and bake for 45 minutes, turning the sausages and potatoes over halfway through. Once everything is cooked through, season to taste, then serve and enjoy!

Easy Butter Chicken AND RICE

PREP TIME: 15 MINUTES, PLUS 30 MINUTES MARINATING (OR OVERNIGHT) | COOKING TIME: 30 MINUTES | SERVES 2
CALORIES: 531 KCAL | CARBS: 50G | FAT: 13G | PROTEIN: 43G

If you're after a quick and simple curry recipe, then this is the one for you! I love a classic butter chicken, and this one is so easy to make. It's the perfect curry to try if you've not yet cooked one from scratch!

Ingredients

For the marinated chicken

2 large chicken breasts, diced
1 tbsp turmeric
1 tbsp garlic salt
1 tbsp mild curry powder
2 tsp ground ginger
2 tsp ground cumin
1 tbsp lemon juice

For the curry

20g light butter
4 cloves of garlic, minced
1 onion, diced
1 tsp ground ginger
1 tsp garam masala
1 tbsp tomato purée
80ml chicken stock
50ml double cream
200g rice, to serve (microwaveable, if preferred)
1 tsp dried coriander, to garnish

Method

Combine the chicken with the marinade ingredients and leave to marinate in the fridge for at least 30 minutes but ideally overnight.

Melt the butter in a pan and add the garlic and onion, frying for a few minutes until fragrant. Season with ground ginger and garam masala, then add the tomato purée and marinated chicken breast. Fry the chicken for about 10 minutes until it's cooked through.

Pour in the chicken stock and double cream and reduce to a simmer to allow the sauce to thicken, about 15 minutes. Serve with rice and garnish with a sprinkling of dried coriander!

Sausage and RED PESTO PASTA

PREP TIME: 10 MINUTES | COOKING TIME: 20 MINUTES | SERVES 2
CALORIES: 632 KCAL | CARBS: 74G | FAT: 28G | PROTEIN: 20G

This is one of those quick and easy pasta dishes that's perfect for when you've had a busy day and just want something comforting and delicious. It only takes 30 minutes and it's SO good.

Ingredients

180g dried penne pasta
1 tsp olive oil
4 cloves of garlic, minced
1 onion, diced
4 chipolata sausages, chopped and skin removed
Pinch of salt and pepper
2 tsp dried oregano
2 tsp paprika
2 tsp dried basil
150ml chicken stock
50ml double cream
1 heaped tbsp red pesto
10g parmesan, grated
2 tsp dried parsley

Method

Cook the pasta as per the packet instructions. Meanwhile, heat a teaspoon of olive oil in a pan with the chopped garlic and onion and fry for a couple minutes until fragrant. Add the chopped sausages and fry for 5 to 7 minutes until the sausage begins to brown. Season with salt, pepper, oregano, paprika and basil.

Pour in the chicken stock, followed by the double cream and red pesto. Stir until combined, then leave to simmer on a low to medium heat to allow the sauce to reduce and thicken.

Finish by stirring through the cooked pasta and grated parmesan, then garnish with a sprinkle of dried parsley.

Budget Meal Plan
WEEK FOUR

5 MEALS FOR TWO FOR £30

SHOPPING LIST

From The Shop

4 x 5% fat beef burgers
1 pack of bacon medallions
650g chicken breasts (medium pack)
1 bag frozen garlic and herb prawns (200g)
Reduced fat soft cheese
Grated mozzarella
Grated parmesan
Packet of fresh gnocchi
White onions
Maris Piper potatoes
Cherry tomatoes
Carton of tomato passata
Tomato purée
1 jar of green pesto
2 brioche burger buns
Dried spaghetti

Note:

If garlic and herb prawns aren't available, you can make your own! Make garlic butter by combining 10g melted butter, 10g garlic paste and 2 teaspoons of dried parsley, then use it to coat the prawns before cooking.

From The Kitchen

Olive oil
Sunflower oil
Lemon juice
Worcestershire sauce
Apple cider vinegar
Burger sauce
BBQ sauce
Golden breadcrumbs
Vegetable stock cubes
Salt
Pepper
Dried parsley
Mixed Italian herbs
Garlic salt
Paprika
BBQ seasoning
Chilli flakes

BBQ Bacon Double Cheeseburgers AND SKIN-ON FRIES

PREP TIME: 10 MINUTES | COOKING TIME: 30 MINUTES | SERVES 2
CALORIES: 640 KCAL (EXCLUDING THE FRIES) | CARBS: 56G | FAT: 25G | PROTEIN: 61G

Make burger night a weekly staple with these tasty AND high protein BBQ bacon burgers! One of my favourite tips when making burgers is to wrap them in tin foil and pop them into the oven for a few minutes. It makes all the difference!

Ingredients

For the fries

3-4 Maris Piper potatoes
Pinch of salt and pepper
1 tsp garlic salt
1 tsp paprika
1 tbsp olive oil

For the burgers

4 x 5% fat beef burgers
1 tsp sunflower oil
Pinch of salt and pepper
4 bacon medallions
2 brioche burger buns
1 tbsp burger sauce
40g grated mozzarella
4 tbsp BBQ sauce

Method

To make the skin-on fries, slice the potatoes into fries but leave the skin on. Add to a bowl and season with salt, pepper, garlic salt, paprika and oil then transfer to the air fryer for 20 minutes at 200°c, or to a preheated oven for 30 minutes at 200°c.

Meanwhile, to make the burgers, start by preheating the grill. Place the burger patties onto a lightly oiled baking tray and, using the back of a spatula, squish each burger until they become nice and flat. Season with some salt and pepper, then transfer to the grill and cook for about 5 minutes less than the time stated on the packet.

While the burgers are cooking, fry the bacon until cooked to your preference. Slice the brioche buns in half and spread half a tablespoon of burger sauce over the base of each.

Just before the burgers are ready to come out, sprinkle the grated mozzarella over two of them and grill for a couple more minutes. Once the cheese has melted, add one of the cheesy burgers to a brioche base, then layer with 1 tablespoon of BBQ sauce, a second burger patty, 2 bacon medallions, and another tablespoon of BBQ sauce. Top with the brioche bun lid then repeat with the second burger.

You can loosely wrap the burgers in tin foil and pop them into the air fryer for around 5 minutes at this stage, if preferred. This gives the burgers that fast food taste and melts all of those delicious ingredients together.

Once cooked to your preference, serve the burgers with the skin-on fries and your favourite dip!

Hot Honey PIZZA-TOPPED CHICKEN

PREP TIME: 10 MINUTES | COOKING TIME: 30 MINUTES | SERVES 2
CALORIES: 400 KCAL | CARBS: 16G | FAT: 17G | PROTEIN: 44G

Prepared in one dish, this cheesy pizza-topped chicken is delicious. It even comes with a drizzle of hot honey for an extra kick!

Ingredients

1 tbsp oil
2 chicken breasts
Pinch of salt and pepper
1 tbsp mixed Italian herbs
1 tbsp garlic salt
1 tsp dried oregano
2 tsp paprika
400g tomato passata
2 tbsp tomato purée
60g grated mozzarella
6 slices pepperoni
1 tbsp honey
2 tsp chilli flakes

Method

Preheat the oven to 200°c. Add the chicken to an oven dish with a tablespoon of oil. Season the chicken with salt and pepper, Italian herbs, garlic salt, oregano, and paprika, then pour in the tomato passata and tomato purée and give it a good mix.

Transfer to the oven and bake for 20 minutes. Remove, then top the chicken with the grated mozzarella and pepperoni slices. Combine the honey and chilli flakes, then drizzle the chicken with the hot honey mix before returning it to the oven for a further 5 to 7 minutes.

Once the cheese has turned a nice golden-brown colour and the sauce is bubbling, it's ready to serve with potato wedges and/or a side salad.

Hunter's Chicken LOADED FRIES

PREP TIME: 10 MINUTES | COOKING TIME: 45 MINUTES | SERVES 2
CALORIES: 548 KCAL | CARBS: 47G | FAT: 16G | PROTEIN: 60G

If you love a classic Hunter's Chicken and you love loaded fries, then this combo is sure to go down well! The delicious BBQ chicken is served on top of homemade fries with crispy bacon bits and grated mozzarella cheese. Comfort in a dish for less than 600 calories!

Ingredients

For the fries

3-4 Maris Piper potatoes
1 tbsp olive oil
Pinch of salt and pepper
2 tsp paprika
2 tsp garlic salt

For the hunter's chicken

2 chicken breasts
1 tsp paprika
1 tbsp BBQ seasoning
Pinch of salt and pepper
4 tbsp BBQ sauce
2 tbsp Worcestershire sauce
1 tbsp apple cider vinegar
4 bacon medallions, chopped
60g grated mozzarella
1 tsp dried parsley, to garnish

Method

Preheat the oven to 200°c. Chop the potatoes into fries, leaving the skin on, and pop them into a bowl. Add the oil and season with salt, pepper, paprika and garlic salt. Transfer to a large ovenproof dish and pop into the oven to cook for around 30 to 35 minutes until crisp and golden-brown. While the chips are cooking, lay the chicken breasts in an ovenproof dish and season with paprika, BBQ seasoning, and a pinch of salt and pepper. In a small bowl, combine the BBQ sauce, Worcestershire sauce and apple cider vinegar, then pour the sauce over the chicken.

Transfer the chicken breasts into the oven and cook for around 25 minutes. Meanwhile, fry the chopped bacon on a high heat until crispy, then set aside. When the chicken is done, remove it from the oven and use two forks to shred the meat. Stir it around the dish to coat the shredded chicken in the sauce.

When the chips have cooked, top them with the shredded BBQ chicken, chopped bacon bits and grated cheese. Return the baking tray to the oven for a further 5 to 7 minutes until the cheese melts and starts to bubble. Finish with an extra drizzle of BBQ sauce and some dried parsley.

Baked Pesto and MOZZARELLA GNOCCHI

PREP TIME: 10 MINUTES | COOKING TIME: 45 MINUTES | SERVES 2
CALORIES: 545 KCAL | CARBS: 90G | FAT: 12G | PROTEIN: 11G

I love gnocchi, and this baked version is absolutely delicious. The golden breadcrumbs make a delicious crumb and they work super well with the pesto! This is a fab one-dish recipe and it takes just 10 minutes to prepare.

Ingredients

500g fresh gnocchi
Pinch of salt and pepper
1 tbsp garlic salt
2 tbsp reduced fat soft cheese
1 vegetable stock cube, dissolved in 150ml boiling water
250g cherry tomatoes
4 tbsp green pesto
2 tbsp golden breadcrumbs
20g parmesan, grated

Method

Add the gnocchi to an ovenproof dish and season with salt, pepper and garlic salt. Then, add the soft cheese and vegetable stock to a small jug and stir until smooth and combined. Add the creamy stock to the gnocchi with the cherry tomatoes and pesto, then stir everything together so it's fully coated and mixed evenly. Sprinkle the breadcrumbs and parmesan over the top of the gnocchi, then place the dish into the oven for around 40 to 45 minutes until the bake is golden-brown and crispy on top.

Garlic Pesto PRAWN SPAGHETTI

PREP TIME: 10 MINUTES | COOKING TIME: 20 MINUTES | SERVES 2
CALORIES: 560 KCAL | CARBS: 94G | FAT: 7G | PROTEIN: 30G

One of my all-time favourite spaghetti dishes! I buy these frozen prawns from ALDI – they're absolutely delicious and they make for a gorgeous pasta sauce. It's simple but full of flavour and done in 30 minutes!

Ingredients

180g dried spaghetti

1 bag frozen garlic and herb prawns (200g, see notes)

1 white onion, diced

Pinch of salt and pepper

2 tsp mixed Italian herbs

2 tbsp reduced fat soft cheese

2 tsp lemon juice

1 tsp dried parsley

Method

Start by cooking the spaghetti as per the packet instructions. Make sure to reserve some pasta water to add to the sauce later. Meanwhile, in a separate pan, add the bag of frozen prawns to the pan with the onion and begin to fry for around 5 to 7 minutes until the prawns have thawed and start to cook through. Season with some salt, pepper and the mixed Italian herbs.

Add the soft cheese and stir it through until a sauce begins to form, then add the lemon juice. When the spaghetti has cooked, transfer it to the pan with the prawns and toss it through. Add a ladle of pasta water to loosen the sauce, then serve the pasta immediately and garnish with some dried parsley!

Note:

If garlic and herb prawns aren't available, you can make your own! Make garlic butter by combining 10g melted butter, 10g garlic paste and 2 teaspoons of dried parsley, then use it to coat the prawns before cooking.

Lunches & Meal Prep

Have you ever found yourself standing in a supermarket's meal deal section for the fourth time that week thinking: "I wish I'd just made something at home"? If so, it's time to say goodbye to the supermarket sarnies and say hello to your new lunch menu! Here's a whole chapter dedicated to some easy and delicious lunch and meal prep recipes that'll save you time and money. Most of these are designed to be easy to prep the night before and stored in the fridge, so you can grab them and go if you're heading to work or are short on time. There are also a few no-reheat lunch ideas which are ideal if you're on the go with no microwave in sight.

Peri Peri Chicken and HALLOUMI RICE BOWLS

PREP TIME: 10 MINUTES | COOKING TIME: 30 MINUTES | MAKES 3 PORTIONS
CALORIES: 551 KCAL | CARBS: 39G | FAT: 26G | PROTEIN: 43G

This is a great recipe for meal prep as it can be easily prepared in one oven dish! Just portion it up into 3 containers and that's your lunches sorted.

Ingredients

1 tbsp olive oil
200g halloumi, sliced
2 large chicken breasts, diced
2 tbsp peri peri seasoning
Pinch of salt and pepper
2 cloves of garlic, minced
1 tbsp tomato purée
1 red bell pepper, sliced
1 yellow bell pepper, sliced
1 white onion, diced
300g long grain rice
800ml chicken stock
1 tsp fresh parsley, chopped

Method

Heat some oil in a large pan and add the halloumi. Fry on each side for 5 minutes until the halloumi turns a nice golden-brown, then remove and set aside. Add the diced chicken breast to the same pan along with the peri peri seasoning, salt, pepper, and garlic. Fry for around 10 minutes, then add the tomato purée, sliced peppers and onion. Fry until the chicken is completely cooked through and golden.

Add the rice and chicken stock and stir everything together, then cover the pan and cook for 15 minutes until the rice has absorbed the stock. Add the halloumi back in for a couple minutes to warm through, then garnish with some fresh parsley.

Note:

Pop into three meal prep containers and store in the fridge for up to 3 days. To reheat, microwave for 3 and a half minutes, stirring halfway through, until it's piping hot throughout.

Sweet Chilli CHICKEN BAGEL

PREP TIME: 5 MINUTES | COOKING TIME: 10 MINUTES | SERVES 1
CALORIES: 432 KCAL | CARBS: 24G | FAT: 8G | PROTEIN: 13G

Bagels are so easy to make and so delicious, too! You can make this sweet chilli chicken bagel the night before, wrap it in tin foil, and enjoy it cold the next day. It makes a great, easy, on-the-go lunch!

Ingredients

1 chicken breast, diced
Pinch of salt and pepper
1 tsp paprika
1 tsp garlic salt
3 tbsp sweet chilli sauce
2 tsp light soy sauce
2 tbsp mayonnaise
1 tbsp oil
1 tsp garlic paste
1 bagel
1 handful of lettuce, chopped

Method

Add the diced chicken breast to a bowl with the salt, pepper, paprika, garlic salt, 2 tablespoons of sweet chilli sauce, the soy sauce and 1 tablespoon of mayonnaise, and mix well.

Add the oil to a pan with the garlic paste and chicken, then fry off until the chicken is cooked through. While the chicken is cooking, lightly toast the bagel. Just before the chicken has finished cooking, stir in the final tablespoon of sweet chilli sauce.

Spread the remaining mayonnaise onto the bagel then layer with the lettuce and sweet chilli chicken.

Sausage and Pesto Parmesan PASTA SALAD

PREP TIME: 15 MINUTES | COOKING TIME: 20 MINUTES | MAKES 3 PORTIONS
CALORIES: 540 KCAL | CARBS: 65G | FAT: 25G | PROTEIN: 25G

Sausage and pesto just work SO well together, and this pasta salad is the perfect summer lunch idea (or all year round, really!). This one's another easy one-bowl recipe!

Ingredients

250g dried penne pasta
1 tsp olive oil
1 white onion, diced
3 cloves of garlic, diced
6 sausages, chopped and skin removed
4 tbsp basil pesto
1 tbsp reduced fat soft cheese
40g parmesan, grated
2 tsp dried parsley

Method

Cook the pasta as per the packet instructions. While the pasta is cooking, heat a little oil in a pan and add the diced white onion and garlic. Fry for a couple minutes before adding the chopped sausage and frying until browned.

When the pasta is cooked, drain and tip into a large bowl. Add the fried sausage and onion, pesto, and soft cheese and stir to combine. To finish, sprinkle with the grated parmesan cheese and some dried parsley!

Portion up and keep refrigerated for up to 3 days.

Slow Cooker
BEEF AND POTATO CURRY

PREP TIME: 15 MINUTES | COOKING TIME: 4-8 HOURS | MAKES 3 PORTIONS
CALORIES: 595 KCAL | CARBS: 40G | FAT: 17G | PROTEIN: 42G

This one makes such an easy and delicious meal prep. Just throw everything into the slow cooker and portion it up once done! It's easy to reheat the next day and makes a filling, high-protein lunch.

Ingredients

1 tbsp olive oil
500g beef stewing steak
500g new potatoes
2 white onions, diced
1 x 400g tin of chopped tomatoes
200ml coconut milk
2 tbsp tomato purée
6 cloves of garlic, minced
3 tbsp medium curry powder
2 tsp garam masala
4 tsp ground ginger
2 tsp fresh coriander leaf
250g basmati rice, to serve
Fresh coriander, chopped to serve

Method

Warm some oil in a pan and fry the stewing steak for around 3 to 5 minutes. Once browned, transfer the steak and all the ingredients (apart from the rice) into the slow cooker, mixing everything together. Cook for around 4 to 6 hours on high, or 6 to 8 hours on low.

Once cooked, prepare the rice as per the packet instructions. Take three meal prep containers and portion the rice and curry into the containers. Sprinkle with fresh coriander and store in the fridge for up to 3 days.

Note:

To reheat, microwave for 3 minutes, stirring halfway through, until the curry is piping hot throughout.

Pulled BBQ Chicken AND RICE

PREP TIME: 10 MINUTES | COOKING TIME: 25 MINUTES | MAKES 3 PORTIONS
CALORIES: 425 KCAL | CARBS: 44G | FAT: 7G | PROTEIN: 46G

This pulled BBQ chicken is so easy to make! It's done in the oven so it's great if you don't own a slow cooker or are short on time.

Ingredients

1 tsp olive oil
4 chicken breasts
Pinch of salt and pepper
2 tsp garlic salt
2 tsp paprika
2 tsp onion powder
1 tsp ground cumin
2 tbsp BBQ seasoning
200g BBQ sauce
1 tbsp Worcestershire sauce
2 tbsp apple cider vinegar
225g your choice of rice

Method

Preheat the oven to 200°c. Gently warm some oil in the bottom of a hob-safe oven dish over a medium heat for a few minutes. Meanwhile, combine the chicken with the salt, pepper, garlic salt, paprika, onion powder, cumin and BBQ seasoning. In a separate pan, fry the chicken off for a couple minutes until browned, but not cooked through.

In a small bowl, combine the BBQ sauce, Worcestershire sauce and apple cider vinegar. When the chicken has browned, add it to the oven dish and coat the chicken in the sauce. Transfer the chicken to the oven and bake for 20 minutes until the chicken is totally cooked through. While the chicken is cooking, cook the rice as per the packet instructions.

When cooked, remove the chicken from the oven and shred it with two forks, then portion it into three meal prep containers along with the rice. Drizzle an extra tablespoon of BBQ sauce on top and it's ready to pop into the fridge!

Once refrigerated, this'll keep for up to 3 days.

Note:

To reheat, microwave for 3 minutes, stirring halfway through, until piping hot throughout.

Satay Chicken NOODLES

PREP TIME: 10 MINUTES | COOKING TIME: 20 MINUTES | MAKES 3 PORTIONS
CALORIES: 602 KCAL | CARBS: 28G | FAT: 29G | PROTEIN: 52G

Spice up your lunches with this delicious satay chicken noodle bowl! You can easily meal prep this dish as it tastes great when warmed up the next day. Not only does this make a good lunch, but it's a tasty evening meal too – you could always make more and save some for another meal!

Ingredients

For the satay sauce

4 tbsp smooth peanut butter
1 clove of garlic, minced
1 tbsp light soy sauce
6 tbsp coconut milk
1 tbsp lime juice
1 tsp sugar

For the noodles

2 tsp sesame oil
3 large chicken breasts, diced
2 tbsp curry powder (mild, medium or hot depending on preference)
2 tsp light soy sauce
Pinch of salt and pepper
300g egg noodles
2 carrots, grated
2 handfuls of red cabbage, grated
2 spring onions, chopped
1 tsp sesame seeds
1 lime wedge (plus more to garnish, if desired)

Method

In a small bowl, combine the satay sauce ingredients, stirring well to form a smooth sauce, then set aside.

Warm some sesame oil in a pan and add the diced chicken. Season with curry powder, soy sauce, salt and pepper and fry until the chicken is cooked through. Meanwhile, cook the noodles as per the packet instructions.

Add the grated carrot and cabbage to the pan with the chicken and fry for a couple of minutes. Add the cooked, drained noodles and toss everything together. Turn the heat to low and add the satay sauce, stirring it through until the noodles and chicken are fully coated.

Garnish with chopped spring onion, a sprinkle of sesame seeds and a squeeze of lime juice.

Split into three portions and keep in the fridge for up to 3 days.

Note:

To reheat, sprinkle a little water on the noodles, give them a stir, and microwave for around 3 minutes until piping hot throughout. Stir halfway through.

Pesto, Roasted Veg and FETA FLATBREADS

PREP TIME: 10 MINUTES | COOKING TIME: 25 MINUTES | SERVES 2
CALORIES: 426 KCAL | CARBS: 56G | FAT: 18G | PROTEIN: 13G

I love how quick and simple this dish is! You can use all your favourite veg in this dish – just throw it all on a baking tray and get it in the oven! Load up your flatbread and you're good to go.

Ingredients

1 red onion, sliced
1 red bell pepper, sliced
1 yellow bell pepper, sliced
1 tomato, chopped
1 courgette, chopped
6 whole garlic cloves
2 tbsp olive oil
1 tsp salt
1 tsp pepper
2 tsp mixed Italian herbs
2 tsp paprika
2 tsp lemon juice
2 flatbreads (see page 46 for my two-ingredient dough)
4 tsp red pesto
40g feta cheese
2 tsp dried parsley

Method

Preheat the oven to 200°c, then lightly oil a baking tray. Spread the chopped veg onto the tray along with the cloves of garlic, then drizzle with olive oil and season with some salt and pepper, mixed Italian herbs, paprika and lemon juice.

Roast the veg in the oven for around 25 minutes until it's golden-brown and softened.

While the veg is cooking, take the flatbreads and sprinkle them with water on each side, then pop them into the oven for a minute to soften.

Spread a layer of pesto onto the base of each then, then place the roasted vegetables on top of the flatbreads. Finish with a crumbling of feta cheese and the dried parsley before serving!

Red Pesto, Feta and Sun-dried TOMATO PASTA SALAD

PREP TIME: 10 MINUTES | COOKING TIME: 10 MINUTES | MAKES 3 PORTIONS
CALORIES: 523 KCAL | CARBS: 77G | FAT: 17G | PROTEIN: 18G

This pasta salad just screams summer! I'm a big pesto lover myself and I love it even more in pasta. This makes a great side for summer barbecues or an easy meal prep for work lunches!

Ingredients

250g dried penne pasta
4 tbsp red pesto
50g reduced fat soft cheese
2 tbsp mayonnaise
2 tsp garlic paste
1 tbsp lemon juice
1 tsp dried parsley
60g feta cheese, diced
100g sun-dried tomatoes
Fresh basil, to garnish
1 tsp parmesan, grated, to garnish

Method

Begin by cooking the pasta as per the packet instructions.

Once cooked, set aside in a large mixing bowl to cool. In a small dish, mix the red pesto, soft cheese, mayonnaise, garlic, lemon juice and parsley and stir to form the dressing.

Add the feta cheese and sun-dried tomatoes to the pasta, followed by the pesto dressing, then stir to coat.

Garnish with fresh basil and grated parmesan.

Portion up and keep in the fridge for up to 4 days.

Lime and Coconut CHICKPEA CURRY AND RICE

PREP TIME: 10 MINUTES | COOKING TIME: 25 MINUTES | MAKES 3 PORTIONS
CALORIES: 493 KCAL | CARBS: 52G | FAT: 29G | PROTEIN: 13G

This chickpea curry is the perfect lunch idea for meal prep. It's budget friendly, all cooked in one pan, and easily stored in the fridge! What's not to love?

Ingredients

1 tbsp oil
1 white onion, diced
4 cloves of garlic, minced
1 x 400g tin of chopped tomatoes
1 tsp ground cumin
1 tsp garam masala
2 tsp medium curry powder
1 x 400g tin of chickpeas
300ml coconut milk
1 tbsp lime juice
Pinch of salt and pepper
250g basmati rice
Fresh coriander, to garnish

Method

Heat a tablespoon of oil in a large pan. Add the diced onion and garlic and fry for a couple of minutes until fragrant. Then, add the chopped tomatoes followed by the cumin, garam masala and curry powder, stirring everything together before reducing to a simmer.

Drain the chickpeas and add them to the pan, followed by the coconut milk and lime juice. Season with salt and pepper to taste. Leave the curry on a low to medium simmer to allow the sauce to reduce for around 10 minutes.

Meanwhile, prepare the rice and portion it into three meal prep containers. When the curry is ready, garnish it with some fresh coriander and add it to the meal prep containers along with the rice.

Note:

Keep refrigerated for up to 4 days. To reheat, pop in the microwave for 3 to 4 minutes, stirring halfway through, until it's piping hot throughout.

KFC Rice Box FAKEAWAY

PREP TIME: 10 MINUTES | COOKING TIME: 15 MINUTES | SERVES 2
CALORIES: 484 KCAL | CARBS: 46G | FAT: 14G | PROTEIN: 42G

If you're a KFC lover then you need to try this homemade version of a rice box! It's so simple to make but so delicious – and it takes less than 30 minutes.

Ingredients

25g panko breadcrumbs
1 tsp garlic granules
1 tsp onion powder
1 tsp paprika
1 tsp dried oregano
1 tsp dried thyme
Pinch of salt and pepper
1 large egg
2 chicken breasts
1 tsp olive oil, or spray oil
1 pack of chicken-flavoured microwave rice
1 handful of lettuce, chopped
1 handful of cherry tomatoes, halved
¼ cucumber, chopped
1 tsp dried parsley
2 tbsp sriracha mayonnaise

Method

Combine the panko breadcrumbs with the dried herbs and spices (excluding the parsley) and spread them out on a plate. Crack the egg into a bowl and whisk until beaten. Dip a chicken breast into the egg and then coat it in the breadcrumb mix. Repeat with the second chicken breast.

Spray or drizzle with oil, then pop the chicken into an air fryer for 15 minutes at 180°c, or into a preheated oven at 180°c for 20 to 25 minutes.

To prepare the rest of the rice box, microwave the rice as per the packet instruction and place in the bottom of a tub or bowl. Add the lettuce, tomatoes, cucumber, and any other salad ingredients you fancy (like sliced onion or sweetcorn). When the chicken is cooked through, slice it horizontally and lay it on top of the rice and salad.

Garnish with a dried parsley and a drizzle of sriracha mayo for an extra kick!

Lemon Halloumi ORZO

PREP TIME: 5 MINUTES | COOKING TIME: 20 MINUTES | MAKES 3 PORTIONS
CALORIES: 466 KCAL | CARBS: 41G | FAT: 24G | PROTEIN: 22G

This recipe is the perfect summer dish! Gorgeous as a barbecue side or an easy, no-reheat lunch (because it tastes even better chilled!).

Ingredients

280g dried orzo
1 tbsp olive oil
2 tsp dried parsley
3 tbsp lemon juice, plus extra to serve
1 tsp garlic paste
200g halloumi, sliced
200g cherry tomatoes, sliced
1 tbsp basil pesto
1 handful of fresh basil

Method

Cook the orzo pasta as per the packet instructions. Meanwhile, in a small bowl, combine the oil, parsley, lemon juice and garlic, then drizzle it over the halloumi. Fry the halloumi on both sides until crisp and golden.

When the orzo is cooked, drain and transfer to a large bowl. Stir in the tomatoes and pesto, then add the fried halloumi, any remaining oil from the pan, and a little extra lemon juice before garnishing with some fresh basil!

Store any leftovers in the fridge for up to 3 days.

High Protein Chicken and Bacon PINWHEELS

PREP TIME: 5 MINUTES | COOKING TIME: 15 MINUTES | SERVES 1
CALORIES: 493 KCAL | CARBS: 21G | FAT: 24G | PROTEIN: 50G

Pinwheels are such a fun and different way to enjoy a cold wrap for lunch! These chicken and bacon ones are super tasty and really good cold, so you can make them the night before and enjoy them the next day.

Ingredients

1 tsp olive oil
2 tsp garlic paste
1 chicken breast, diced
Pinch of salt and pepper
2 tsp paprika
2 tsp dried oregano
2 bacon medallions, chopped
30g reduced fat soft cheese
1 tbsp light mayonnaise
15g grated mozzarella
1 tortilla wrap

Method

Warm the oil in a frying pan then add the garlic and fry off for a couple of minutes. Add the diced chicken breast and season with salt, pepper, paprika and oregano.

Fry off for around 5 minutes, then add the chopped bacon medallions and fry everything together. When the chicken and bacon have cooked through, transfer them to a small bowl. Stir in the soft cheese, mayonnaise and mozzarella, mixing until combined. Leave the pan on a very low heat to stay warm.

Place the mixture in the middle of a tortilla wrap and roll it into a burrito. Transfer the wrap to a clean pan and fry off on each side for a few minutes to seal it, then leave to cool completely in the fridge.

When the wrap has cooled, slice it into equal bite-sized pieces. You can keep the pinwheels refrigerated and enjoy them the next day, too!

Fajita Chicken POTATO SALAD

PREP TIME: 5 MINUTES, PLUS COOLING TIME | COOKING TIME: 20 MINUTES | MAKES 3 PORTIONS
CALORIES: 344 KCAL | CARBS: 42G | FAT: 11G | PROTEIN: 24G

Spice up your usual potato salad with this fajita-style twist! This is the perfect meal prep for an easy lunch or you can serve it on the side at your next summer barbecue.

Ingredients

500g salad potatoes
1 tsp olive oil
1 tbsp garlic paste
1 red onion, sliced
1 red bell pepper, chopped
1 yellow bell pepper, chopped
2 large chicken breasts, diced
2 tsp salt
2 tsp pepper
3 tsp paprika
2 tbsp fajita seasoning
4 tbsp mayonnaise
2 tbsp reduced fat soft cheese
1 tbsp sour cream
1 spring onion, diced

Method

Add the potatoes to a pan of boiling water and cook until you can stick a fork into them without too much pressure (but not too easily, either!). When the potatoes have cooked, drain and set aside to cool in a large mixing bowl. Heat the oil in a pan with the garlic, then add the chopped onion and peppers and fry off for a couple of minutes until they begin to soften. Then, add the diced chicken breast followed by the salt, pepper, paprika and fajita seasoning. Fry on a medium heat for 7 to 10 minutes until the chicken has cooked through.

Add the fajita chicken mix to the cooked potatoes and toss everything together. Stir in the mayonnaise, reduced fat soft cheese and sour cream, then season to taste with more salt, pepper, and fajita seasoning.

Finish with a sprinkling of paprika and the chopped spring onion, then leave to cool in the fridge! It'll stay fresh for 3 days if refrigerated.

Crispy Potato SALAD

PREP TIME: 10 MINUTES | COOKING TIME: 1 HOUR | SERVES 2
CALORIES: 364 KCAL | CARBS: 18G | FAT: 9G | PROTEIN: 10G

Level up your normal potato salad with this crispy version! This is one of my favourite things to make for a tasty lunch or, even better, a gorgeous side for a barbecue!

Ingredients

400g new potatoes
Pinch of salt and pepper
2 tsp garlic salt
4 tsp paprika
2 tsp olive oil
4 tbsp 0% authentic Greek yoghurt
3 tsp lemon juice, (plus two lemon wedges to serve)
2 tsp Dijon mustard
2 tsp white wine vinegar
2 cloves of garlic, minced
2 tsp dried parsley
½ cucumber, diced
1 spring onion, diced
1 tsp fresh parsley, chopped
2 lemon wedges

Method

Preheat the oven to 200°c. Bring a pan of water to the boil and add the potatoes, boiling for around 5 minutes until the potatoes have slightly softened. Line a baking tray with some tin foil, spraying lightly with oil, then transfer the potatoes to the baking tray. Season with salt, pepper, garlic salt, 2 teaspoons of paprika and a drizzle of oil, and bake for 30 minutes. Remove from the oven and, using the base of a glass, smash each potato. Return to the oven for a further 20 minutes until the potatoes are super crispy and golden-brown.

While the potatoes are cooking, combine the Greek yoghurt, lemon juice, mustard, vinegar, garlic, dried parsley and the remaining paprika to make a smooth dressing.

When the potatoes have cooled, add them to a large bowl with the cucumber and onion, then pour over the dressing and stir until combined. Garnish with fresh parsley and a squeeze of lemon juice. Portion up any leftovers and keep refrigerated for up to 3 days.

Creamy CAJUN PASTA

PREP TIME: 10 MINUTES | COOKING TIME: 20 MINUTES | MAKES 3 PORTIONS
CALORIES: 575 KCAL | CARBS: 66G | FAT: 14G | PROTEIN: 45G

One of my favourite pasta dishes of all time! This Creamy Cajun Pasta makes the perfect meal prep or evening meal. Adjust the seasoning to your spice preference as it does have a bit of a kick!

Ingredients

280g dried penne pasta
1 tbsp olive oil
2 cloves of garlic, minced
1 white onion, diced
1 red bell pepper, sliced
1 yellow bell pepper, sliced
Pinch of salt and pepper
2 tsp paprika
2 tsp dried oregano
3 tbsp Cajun seasoning
3 large chicken breasts, diced
2 tsp garlic salt
2 tsp tomato purée
150ml chicken stock
70g reduced fat soft cheese
20g parmesan, grated
2 tsp dried parsley
Fresh parsley, to garnish (optional)

Method

Begin by cooking the pasta as per the packet instructions. Make sure to reserve some of the pasta water to use for the sauce. While the pasta is cooking, warm a little olive oil in a pan and fry the garlic for a couple of minutes. Add the diced white onion and fry off for a further few minutes until it becomes translucent, then add the sliced peppers. Season the peppers with the salt, pepper, 1 teaspoon of paprika, 1 teaspoon of oregano and 1 tablespoon of Cajun seasoning and fry on a low to medium heat until softened.

Season the chicken breasts with salt, pepper, 1 tablespoon of Cajun seasoning, garlic salt, and the remaining paprika and oregano. Spray with olive oil, then transfer to the air fryer and cook at 180°c for 15 minutes or until the chicken is cooked through.

When the vegetables have softened, add the tomato purée, chicken stock and soft cheese and leave on a low simmer until it thickens into a sauce. When the pasta has cooked, stir it through the sauce along with a ladle of the reserved pasta water. Leave to simmer for a few minutes to thicken and stir in the final tablespoon of Cajun seasoning. Finally, stir through the parmesan cheese and dried parsley.

Add the pasta to three meal prep containers and add the chicken breast on top. If there's any remaining sauce in the pan, pour this over the top. Garnish with some fresh parsley and pop in the fridge. This one'll keep fresh for up to 3 days!

Note:

To reheat, microwave for 3 minutes, stirring halfway through, until piping hot throughout.

Chipotle Bacon PASTA SALAD

PREP TIME: 5 MINUTES | COOKING TIME: 15 MINUTES | MAKES 3 PORTIONS
CALORIES: 450 KCAL | CARBS: 70G | FAT: 9G | PROTEIN: 22G

Pasta salads are some of my favourite things to have for lunch because they're so easy to meal prep! You can throw everything into a big bowl, and they taste great hot and cold. This Chipotle Bacon Pasta Salad is packed with flavour and has a tiny kick to it!

Ingredients

1 tsp olive oil
6 bacon medallions, chopped
1 red onion, diced
Pinch of salt and pepper
1 tsp garlic paste
1 tsp paprika
250g dried short pasta, such as penne, fusilli, or macaroni
Lime juice, to serve
Dried parsley, to garnish

For the chipotle sauce

4 tbsp chipotle paste
2 tbsp mayonnaise
1 tbsp honey
1 tbsp sour cream
2 tsp lime juice
½ tsp ground cumin
1 tsp paprika
Pinch of salt and pepper

Method

Heat the oil in a pan and add the chopped bacon, red onion, salt, pepper, garlic paste and paprika. Fry until the bacon has cooked through and the onion has softened. Meanwhile, cook the pasta as per the packet instructions and, when done, drain and transfer to a large bowl to cool.

In a small bowl, combine the chipotle sauce ingredients until they form a smooth sauce. Add the fried bacon and onion to the pasta, then stir in the chipotle sauce until everything is well coated.

Finish with a squeeze or dash of lime juice and a sprinkling of dried parsley. Portion up and refrigerate for up to 4 days.

GRANDESSA
Squeezy
HONEY

Chicken Noodle STIR FRY

PREP TIME: 10 MINUTES | COOKING TIME: 20 MINUTES | MAKES 3 PORTIONS
CALORIES: 386 KCAL | CARBS: 40G | FAT: 8G | PROTEIN: 40G

I love this stir fry recipe because of how easy it is to prepare for an easy take-to-work lunch. It's so quick to make but so delicious, too. Plus, coming in at less than 400 calories and 40g of protein a portion, it makes for a nutritious lunch too.

Ingredients

For the stir fry sauce

3 tbsp light soy sauce
3 cloves of garlic, minced
2 tbsp oyster sauce
1 tbsp lime juice
1 tbsp rice wine vinegar

For the stir fry

300g egg noodles
2 tsp sesame oil
3 chicken breasts, diced
1 tsp garlic paste
1 tsp ground ginger
1 tsp chilli flakes (optional)
1 red bell pepper, sliced
1 handful of mushrooms
1 handful of mangetout
4 spring onions, sliced
2 tsp sesame seeds

Method

Combine the soy sauce, garlic, oyster sauce, lime juice and rice wine vinegar, and set aside. Meanwhile, cook the noodles as per the packet instructions.

In a large pan or wok, heat a little sesame oil. Add the diced chicken, garlic and the ginger and fry until the chicken turns a nice golden-brown. Add the chilli flakes here too if you like a kick! When the chicken is cooked, remove it from the pan and set aside.

In the same pan, add the sliced red pepper and fry for a couple minutes. Add the mushrooms, mangetout and three quarters of the spring onion, and fry for another minute. Return the chicken to the pan along with the cooked noodles and stir fry sauce.

Stir everything together and divide into three meal prep containers. Garnish with sesame seeds and the remaining spring onion.

Note:

Keep in the fridge for up to 4 days. To reheat, microwave for 3 and a half minutes, stirring halfway through. Make sure it's piping hot throughout before serving.

Chicken Shawarma PITTAS

PREP TIME: 10 MINUTES, PLUS 30 MINUTES MARINATING (OR OVERNIGHT) | COOKING TIME: 30 MINUTES | SERVES 2
CALORIES: 448 KCAL | CARBS: 44G | FAT: 16G | PROTEIN: 41G

These Middle Eastern-style pittas are one of my absolute fave lunches! They don't just taste amazing, but they're also really easy to make. I'm a huge fan of anything that includes tzatziki; it always brings the best summer vibes.

Ingredients

2 large chicken breasts
1 tbsp garlic powder
¾ tbsp paprika
¾ tbsp turmeric
¾ tbsp ground cumin
Pinch of salt and pepper
1 tbsp lemon juice
1 tsp olive oil
1 red onion, chopped
1 red bell pepper, sliced
1 yellow bell pepper, sliced
2 pitta breads
2 tbsp tzatziki
1 handful of salad leaves
1 handful of cherry tomatoes, halved

Method

Add the chicken breasts to a bowl with the garlic, paprika, turmeric, cumin, salt, pepper, and lemon juice. Stir well and marinate in the fridge for at least 30 minutes, but ideally overnight.

Preheat the oven to 200°c, then lightly oil a baking tray and lay the chicken on top. Add the red onion and bell peppers around the chicken and transfer to the oven. Roast for about 25 minutes or until the chicken and veg are cooked through, then tear up the chicken.

While the chicken is cooking, spread a layer of tzatziki inside the pitta breads and add the salad leaves and chopped tomatoes. Fill each pitta with the chicken and roasted veg and enjoy!

Chicken Caesar PASTA SALAD

PREP TIME: 10 MINUTES | COOKING TIME: 10 MINUTES | MAKES 3 PORTIONS
CALORIES: 515 KCAL | CARBS: 66G | FAT: 9G | PROTEIN: 38G

A pasta salad is one of my favourite things to meal prep because it keeps you fuller for longer and it tastes amazing cold! There are so many variations of pasta salad, but this Caesar-style one is a firm fave.

Ingredients

250g dried penne pasta
250g chicken breasts, cooked
4 handfuls of romaine lettuce, chopped
2 tbsp mayonnaise
1 tbsp Dijon mustard
1 tbsp Worcestershire sauce
2 tbsp lemon juice
3 cloves of garlic, minced
1 tsp olive oil
Pinch of salt and pepper
25g parmesan, grated
1 handful of croutons

Method

Begin by cooking the pasta as per the packet instructions. When the pasta has cooked, drain and set aside to cool in a large mixing bowl. When it has cooled, add the cooked chicken and romaine lettuce, tossing everything together.

In a small bowl, make the Caesar dressing by mixing the mayonnaise, Dijon mustard, Worcestershire sauce, lemon juice, garlic, olive oil, salt and pepper.

Pour this mixture over the pasta and toss to coat, then finish with the grated parmesan and crunchy croutons! Portion the pasta salad into three servings and keep refrigerated for up to 3 days.

Cheesy Meatball PASTA BAKE

PREP TIME: 10 MINUTES | COOKING TIME: 25 MINUTES | MAKES 3 PORTIONS
CALORIES: 580 KCAL | CARBS: 82G | FAT: 10G | PROTEIN: 40G

If you're looking for an easy, simple dish for this week's meal prep then look no further! This cheesy meatball pasta bake is perfect for chucking into the oven and serving up as lunches throughout the week! I often buy a pack of 5% fat meatballs as they're lean, delicious, and perfect for throwing into dishes like these.

Ingredients

1 tsp olive oil
12 x 5% fat beef meatballs
Pinch of salt and pepper
250g dried short pasta, like penne or macaroni
400g tomato passata
2 tbsp tomato purée
1 tbsp garlic paste
2 tsp mixed Italian herbs
2 tsp paprika
1 tsp sugar
150ml water
80g grated mozzarella
2 tsp dried or fresh parsley

Method

Preheat the oven to 180°c and oil an oven dish. Add the meatballs, season with salt and pepper, and transfer to the oven to cook for about 15 minutes until they begin to brown. While the meatballs are cooking, cook the pasta as per the packet instructions. When the pasta has cooked, set aside to cool.

Take the meatballs out of the oven and add the tomato passata, tomato purée, garlic paste, mixed Italian herbs, paprika, sugar, and water. Stir everything through, then pop the dish back into the oven for 10 minutes.

When the meatballs and sauce have nearly cooked through, stir in the cooked pasta, making sure to coat it well with the sauce. Sprinkle the grated mozzarella over the top and bake for a further 3 to 5 minutes or until the cheese is golden and bubbling. Garnish with parsley.

Leave the meatball bake to cool, then portion into three meal prep containers. Leave in the fridge for up to 3 days!

Note:

To reheat, microwave for 3 minutes, stirring halfway through, until piping hot throughout.

Beef Taco SALAD BOWL

PREP TIME: 10 MINUTES | COOKING TIME: 15 MINUTES | MAKES 3 PORTIONS
CALORIES: 390 KCAL | CARBS: 12G | FAT: 17G | PROTEIN: 44G

If you fancy a different way to enjoy a salad, then this beef taco salad is for you! You can add as many different ingredients as you fancy, and it makes for a great filling lunch that you can meal prep beforehand. It doesn't even need reheating – bonus!

Ingredients

500g 5% fat beef mince
Pinch of salt and pepper
2 tsp paprika
2 tsp garlic salt
1 tbsp fajita seasoning
2 handfuls of lettuce, sliced
1 red onion, diced
100g cherry tomatoes, halved
65g cheddar cheese, grated
2 tbsp tomato salsa
2 tbsp sour cream

Method

Fry the beef mince in a pan until it begins to brown, making sure to break it up with a spatula while it cooks.

Season with salt, pepper, paprika, garlic salt and fajita seasoning and fry until it's completely cooked through. Add it to a large mixing bowl and set aside to cool.

Once cooled, add the lettuce, onion, tomatoes, grated cheese, salsa and sour cream to the bowl with the mince. Serve up or portion into three meal prep containers and keep refrigerated for up to 3 days!

Air Fryer Hot Honey PIZZA TOAST

PREP TIME: 5 MINUTES | COOKING TIME: 7 MINUTES | SERVES 2
CALORIES: 295 KCAL | CARBS: 38G | FAT: 12G | PROTEIN: 10G

This is a great idea for whenever you want a simple lunch without any faff. It's nice, easy and ready in about 10 minutes! The honey and pepperoni work so well together too.

Ingredients

1 tbsp olive oil
1 tbsp tomato purée
2 tbsp tomato passata
1 tsp salt
1 tsp pepper
2 tsp garlic salt
2 tsp dried oregano
1 tsp dried thyme
1 tsp dried basil
1 tsp dried parsley
2 slices sourdough bread
30g grated mozzarella
4 slices pepperoni
1 tbsp honey
1 tsp chilli flakes

Method

In a small bowl, combine the olive oil, tomato purée, tomato passata, salt, pepper, garlic, and dried herbs. Spread this over the bread, then top with the grated mozzarella and pepperoni slices.

In another small bowl, add the honey and a teaspoon of chilli flakes (or more if you can handle the heat!). Drizzle this over the top of the pizza toast and pop them in the air fryer at 180°c for around 5 to 7 minutes until the cheese has turned a nice golden-brown and the bread is crispy!

What's for Tea?

Whether you call it dinner or tea (it's tea btw), this chapter will give you some fab inspo for your evening meals. It includes some of my fave, fuss-free, cheap and simple recipes, and they're all less than 650 cals. Winner winner... whatever you make from this chapter for dinner! There's everything from my super popular two-ingredient pizza dough to delicious creamy pastas and drool-worthy burgers. So, if you're stuck on what to have for your tea, give this chapter a quick flick through and you'll be sure to find something delicious.

Italian MEATBALL CALZONES

PREP TIME: 10 MINUTES | COOKING TIME: 50 MINUTES | SERVES 2
CALORIES: 650 KCAL | CARBS: 83G | FAT: 16G | PROTEIN: 51G

The perfect weekend fakeaway recipe! I'm a huge fan of using this two-ingredient dough as it's so easy to make, is high in protein, and makes the perfect base for pizzas, flatbreads and – in this case – calzones!

Ingredients

12 x 5% fat meatballs
180g 0% authentic Greek yoghurt
170g self-raising flour
1 tsp olive oil
1 red onion, diced
2 cloves of garlic, minced
1 tbsp mixed Italian herbs
2 tsp paprika
1 tbsp tomato purée
400g tomato passata
Pinch of salt and pepper
70g grated mozzarella
2 tsp dried parsley
10g garlic paste
10g butter, room temperature

Method

Preheat the oven to 180°c. Put the meatballs in a baking tray and cook them in the oven for 20 minutes. While the meatballs are cooking, add the Greek yoghurt and the self-raising flour to a large mixing bowl. Mix with a spoon until it forms a crumbly texture, then mould the dough into a large ball with your hands. Separate the dough into two equal-sized balls, then lightly flour a flat surface. Roll each dough ball out as flat and as thin as you can, then transfer them to a baking tray.

Heat a teaspoon of oil in a pan, add the chopped onion and garlic, and fry for 3 to 5 minutes until fragrant. Season with the mixed Italian herbs and paprika, then add the tomato purée and tomato passata. Turn down to a simmer for 5 to 7 minutes and season with salt and pepper to taste.

When the meatballs are cooked, stir them into the sauce and simmer together for a couple of minutes. Divide the meatballs between the rolled-out dough, making sure to just cover one side of the dough. Top with the grated mozzarella and 1 teaspoon of dried parsley, then fold the other side of the dough over the top to form the calzone, pressing down at the edges to secure the filling.

In a small dish, combine the garlic paste, butter and remaining dried parsley, then brush it over each calzone. Transfer the calzones to the oven to bake for 15 to 20 minutes until golden-brown!

Creamy
OVEN BAKED CHICKEN

PREP TIME: 10 MINUTES | COOKING TIME: 25 MINUTES | SERVES 2
CALORIES: 620 KCAL | CARBS: 70G | FAT: 17G | PROTEIN: 48G

I can almost guarantee that this easy, budget-friendly chicken dish will become a weekly staple. It's made in one dish with minimal ingredients and goes perfectly with pasta, rice, or potatoes!

Ingredients

1 tbsp olive oil
2 chicken breasts
Pinch of salt and pepper
1 tbsp garlic salt
½ tbsp onion powder
½ tbsp dried oregano
½ tbsp paprika
300ml chicken stock
60g reduced fat soft cheese
2 handfuls of cherry tomatoes
20g parmesan, grated

Method

Preheat the oven to 200°c.

Add a tablespoon of oil to an oven dish and place the chicken breasts inside. Season the chicken on both sides with salt, pepper, garlic salt, onion powder, dried oregano and paprika.

Stir the chicken stock and soft cheese together in a jug until the cheese melts, then pour this over the chicken. Add the cherry tomatoes then sprinkle over the grated parmesan.

Place the chicken in the oven for 20 to 25 minutes until cooked through. Serve with spaghetti, potatoes, or rice and enjoy!

Bang Bang
SALMON BOWL

PREP TIME: 10 MINUTES | COOKING TIME: 20 MINUTES | SERVES 2
CALORIES: 594 KCAL | CARBS: 73G | FAT: 18G | PROTEIN: 32G

Bang bang sauce is one of my favourites. It's made with only three ingredients, and it tastes great on chicken and seafood! I've put it with salmon for this recipe and it's such an easy dinner idea.

Ingredients

5 tbsp sriracha mayonnaise
3 tbsp sweet chilli sauce
2 tbsp honey
2 salmon fillets
Pinch of salt and pepper
1 tsp garlic salt
200g jasmine rice
½ cucumber, grated

Method

Preheat the oven to 180°c. In a small bowl, combine the sriracha mayonnaise, sweet chilli sauce and honey. Place the salmon fillets on a baking tray and season with salt, pepper and garlic salt.

Spread half the bang bang sauce over the salmon fillets and place them into the oven for 15 to 20 minutes.

Meanwhile, cook the rice as per the packet instructions, then add the cooked rice and grated cucumber to a bowl. When the salmon has cooked, discard the skin before cutting it into small chunks and adding it to the bowl with the rice and cucumber.

Pour the rest of the bang bang sauce over the top and serve immediately.

Mexican Taco LOADED FRIES

PREP TIME: 10 MINUTES | COOKING TIME: 35 MINUTES | SERVES 2
CALORIES: 584 KCAL | CARBS: 51G | FAT: 21G | PROTEIN: 52G

One for my Mexican lovers! Delicious beef taco mix and crispy skin-on fries. Unreal! These loaded fries are so simple to make, and – bonus! – they're high in protein so they're super macro-friendly too.

Ingredients

For the fries

3-4 large baking potatoes, chopped into fries (skin left on)
Pinch of salt and pepper
1 tsp garlic granules
1 tsp paprika

For the taco topping

500g 5% fat beef mince
1 tsp Cajun seasoning
1 tsp garlic granules
1 tsp paprika
1 tsp dried oregano
1 tsp onion powder
1 tsp chilli flakes
Pinch of salt and pepper, to taste
4 single cheese slices
1 red onion, diced
1 spring onion, diced
1 tomato, diced
1 tbsp sour cream

Method

Add the chopped fries to a bowl and season with salt, pepper, garlic granules and paprika. Spray well with oil, then pop into the oven at 220°c or an air fryer at 200°c for 25 to 30 minutes.

While the fries are cooking, add the beef mince to a hot pan. Season with the Cajun seasoning, garlic granules, paprika, oregano, onion powder, chilli flakes, salt and pepper, then fry off until the beef is cooked through.

When the fries are golden-brown and crispy, transfer to a large baking tray and top with the cooked beef mince. Take the cheese slices, tear them into small chunks, and scatter them evenly over the top.

Return to the oven or air fryer for 5 to 10 minutes until the cheese melts. Remove from the oven and top with the onions, tomato, and sour cream to serve.

High Protein STUFFED CRUST PIZZA

PREP TIME: 20 MINUTES | COOKING TIME: 20 MINUTES | SERVES 1
CALORIES: 593 KCAL | CARBS: 85G | FAT: 16G | PROTEIN: 33G

My favourite fakeaway! Easy to make, high in protein, low in calories and – in my opinion – even better than a takeout. Try it for yourself and I promise you won't make pizza any other way.

Ingredients

95g self-raising flour

85g 0% authentic Greek yoghurt

40g grated mozzarella, plus 20g for the stuffed crust

4 slices pepperoni

For the pizza sauce

2 tbsp tomato passata

1 tsp tomato purée

1 tsp dried basil

1 tsp dried oregano

1 tsp garlic salt

1 tsp paprika

Method

Preheat the oven to 210°c.

Add the flour and yoghurt to a large mixing bowl, then mix the ingredients together with a spoon until they form a crumbly texture. Use your hands to mould the dough into a large ball (if it's a little sticky, just add a sprinkling of flour). Once you've formed the dough ball, place it on a lightly floured surface and roll out to about 5mm.

Place 20g of the mozzarella around the edge of the dough, then fold the dough over to seal in the cheese for the stuffed crust. Transfer the dough to a lightly oiled baking tray.

Make the pizza sauce by combining the passata, purée and dried seasoning, then spread it onto the pizza base. Sprinkle the rest of the grated mozzarella over the top and add the pepperoni (plus any other optional toppings you fancy!).

Transfer to the oven and cook for 20 minutes until the cheese is bubbling and the crust is golden-brown!

Creamy Cajun HALLOUMI SPAGHETTI

PREP TIME: 5 MINUTES | COOKING TIME: 20 MINUTES | SERVES 2
CALORIES: 504 KCAL | CARBS: 49G | FAT: 22G | PROTEIN: 20G

If you fancy a quick and easy meal that's done in less than 30 minutes then this is for you! I love the chicken version of this recipe, but the halloumi one is just as tasty. If you like a bit of spice, feel free to add more Cajun seasoning!

Ingredients

180g dried spaghetti
60g halloumi, sliced
2 tbsp Cajun seasoning
1 tsp olive oil
2 cloves of garlic, minced
1 white onion, diced
Pinch of salt and pepper
1 tsp paprika
1 tbsp tomato purée
100ml chicken stock
60g reduced fat soft cheese
10g parmesan, grated
1 tsp dried parsley

Method

Start by cooking the spaghetti as per the packet instructions. Coat the halloumi slices in 1 teaspoon of Cajun seasoning, then fry them in an oiled pan on each side for 5 minutes or until golden-brown. Remove the slices from the pan and set them aside.

In the same pan, fry the garlic and white onion until fragrant. Season with salt, pepper, paprika and the rest of the Cajun seasoning, then add the tomato purée, stock and soft cheese. Leave on a low to medium heat and simmer for 5 to 7 minutes until the sauce begins to thicken.

Add the halloumi back into the pan then toss the cooked spaghetti through the sauce. If the sauce becomes too thick, just add a tablespoon of the pasta water. To finish, stir through the grated parmesan then garnish with some dried parsley and serve!

Sticky Halloumi and ROASTED VEG KEBABS

PREP TIME: 10 MINUTES | COOKING TIME: 10 MINUTES | SERVES 2
CALORIES: 408 KCAL | CARBS: 86G | FAT: 10G | PROTEIN: 18G

A taste of summer! These halloumi kebabs are absolutely gorgeous and make the perfect easy midweek meal as they only take 25 minutes! These are best served with some soft pittas and a crunchy side salad.

Ingredients

100g halloumi
1 red onion
2 bell peppers
3 tbsp honey
2 tbsp sweet chilli sauce
1 tbsp garlic paste
1 tsp paprika
Pinch of salt and pepper
2 pitta breads

Method

Cut the halloumi, red onion and bell peppers into chunks, then thread onto wooden or metal kebab skewers.

Combine the honey, sweet chilli sauce, garlic paste and paprika in a small bowl. Coat the halloumi skewers with the sauce, then season with salt and pepper.

Put the skewers under the grill for 5 to 10 minutes until the veg and halloumi are a nice golden-brown colour and slightly charred.

Serve your skewers with some warm pitta breads and a refreshing side salad.

Easy CHICKEN GYROS

PREP TIME: 10 MINUTES | COOKING TIME: 30 MINUTES | SERVES 2
CALORIES: 604 KCAL | CARBS: 57G | FAT: 19G | PROTEIN: 50G

These gyros are one of my ultimate dinners! I just love everything about a gyro, plus they're from one of my favourite countries in the world – Greece! I love making these for guests because of how simple they are to make and serve.

Ingredients

100g skin-on fries, frozen or homemade (see page 76)
1 tbsp olive oil
2 large chicken breasts, diced
Pinch of salt and pepper
2 cloves of garlic, minced
1 tbsp dried oregano
1 tbsp paprika
½ tbsp ground cumin
2 flatbreads (see page 46 for my two-ingredient dough)
4 tbsp tzatziki
2 handfuls of lettuce
½ red onion, sliced
1 handful of cherry tomatoes, sliced in half
2 tbsp garlic mayonnaise (optional)

Method

Preheat the oven to 190°c then cook the skin-on fries as per the packet instructions. Oil an oven dish, add the diced chicken, and then season with salt, pepper, garlic, oregano, paprika and cumin. Pop the chicken into the oven for 25 to 30 minutes until cooked through.

While the chicken and fries are cooking, spread a layer of tzatziki over the flatbreads, then add the lettuce, red onion and cherry tomatoes. When the chicken and fries have cooked, layer them on top, then serve the flatbreads with an extra helping of tzatziki and some garlic mayo!

One Pan Italian
SAUSAGE AND PEPPER

PREP TIME: 10 MINUTES | COOKING TIME: 30 MINUTES | SERVES 2
CALORIES: 395 KCAL | CARBS: 15G | FAT: 25G | PROTEIN: 11G

A super delicious one-pan meal! I like to keep dinner time simple, and this one's perfect for those evenings where you don't want to spend ages cooking. Serve this with some rice or potatoes for a delicious and filling midweek dinner.

Ingredients

1 tbsp olive oil
4 cloves of garlic, minced
4 sausages, cut into bite-sized slices
Pinch of salt and pepper
1 tsp paprika
2 tsp dried thyme
1 tbsp mixed Italian herbs
½ red bell pepper, sliced
½ yellow bell pepper, sliced
½ green bell pepper, sliced
1 red onion, sliced
1 tsp fresh parsley, chopped

Method

Heat a tablespoon of oil in a pan and fry the garlic and sliced sausage for 2 to 3 minutes.

Season the sausage with salt, pepper, paprika, dried thyme and mixed Italian herbs. Fry for a further 5 minutes until the sausage begins to brown.

Add the sliced bell peppers and onion and toss everything together. Leave on a low heat to allow the vegetables to soften, then garnish with some fresh parsley.

Serve as is or over rice or pasta!

Tuscan Sausage PASTA

PREP TIME: 10 MINUTES | COOKING TIME: 20 MINUTES | SERVES 2
CALORIES: 580 KCAL | CARBS: 71G | FAT: 20G | PROTEIN: 22G

I always say the simplest pasta dishes are the most delicious, and this is a recipe that proves my theory! Every time I make this for guests it always goes down a winner.

Ingredients

180g dried penne pasta
1 tsp olive oil
2 cloves of garlic, minced
6 chipolata sausages, skin removed and chopped
1 tsp paprika
1 tsp dried oregano
250ml chicken stock
2 tbsp lemon juice
200ml double cream
½ jar sun-dried tomatoes
1 handful of fresh basil
2 handfuls of spinach
Pinch of salt and pepper

Method

Begin by cooking the pasta as per the packet instructions. Then, in a separate pan, heat a teaspoon of oil and fry the garlic and sausages on a medium-high heat until they begin to brown. Season with the paprika and oregano, then add the chicken stock, lemon juice and double cream. Stir everything together and leave the pan on a low to medium simmer for around 5 minutes. Add the sun-dried tomatoes and a little oil from the jar and cook for another couple of minutes.

Stir in the fresh basil and spinach, cooking until wilted, then season with salt and pepper to taste. Stir the pasta through the sauce and simmer for a couple of minutes to warm through. Serve immediately and enjoy!

Slow Cooker
CHICKEN ALFREDO

PREP TIME: 10 MINUTES | COOKING TIME: 2½-4½ HOURS | SERVES 2
CALORIES: 620 KCAL | CARBS: 70G | FAT: 17G | PROTEIN: 48G

If you're anything like me, then you're a real slow cooker fan! This pasta is beautifully creamy, and I love that you can leave it for a couple of hours, too. You just need to throw everything in the slow cooker, then you'll have an amazing creamy pasta ready to enjoy.

Ingredients

2 chicken breasts
250ml chicken stock
100ml double cream
50ml semi-skimmed milk
1 tbsp garlic powder or garlic salt
2 tsp mixed Italian herbs
½ tsp salt
1 tsp black pepper
180g dried rigatoni
25g grated parmesan
Dried parsley, to serve

Method

Add the chicken breasts, chicken stock, double cream, milk, garlic, Italian herbs, salt, and pepper to a slow cooker. Cook on high for 2 hours or on medium for 4 hours. When ready, take the chicken out, shred it with two forks, and set aside.

Add the rigatoni and parmesan to the slow cooker and cook for a further 20 to 25 minutes until the pasta is cooked. Add the shredded chicken back in, stir it through, and leave for another couple of minutes to warm through.

Garnish with an extra sprinkle of parmesan and some dried parsley!

Ultimate Chicken and BACON SMASH BURGERS

PREP TIME: 15 MINUTES | COOKING TIME: 15 MINUTES | SERVES 2
CALORIES: 647 KCAL | CARBS: 39G | FAT: 26G | PROTEIN: 71G

I bet you wouldn't believe these burgers are less than 650 calories. Well, they are, and they're completely unreal, too! Serve with homemade wedges and crunchy coleslaw, and you've got your new fave Friday night fakeaway.

Ingredients

500g 5% fat chicken mince
1 tsp paprika
1 tsp Cajun seasoning
1 tsp garlic salt
1 tsp onion powder
Pinch of salt and pepper
1 tbsp breadcrumbs
4 bacon medallions
4 single cheese slices
2 brioche burger buns
1 handful of lettuce, chopped
1 red onion, sliced

For the spicy sauce

1 tbsp sriracha mayo
2 tsp sweet chilli sauce
1 tsp sour cream
1 tsp paprika
1 tsp garlic paste

Method

Add the chicken mince to a large mixing bowl and season with the paprika, Cajun seasoning, garlic salt, onion powder, and salt and pepper. Add the breadcrumbs, combine, then portion into four equal-sized balls.

Preheat a grill and cook the bacon to your preference. Meanwhile, preheat a little oil in a pan, then add the chicken burgers and smash them down with the back of a spatula. Cook for 4 to 5 minutes on each side.

Place a cheese slice on each burger patty and leave for a few minutes until the cheese begins to melt.

To build the burger, mix all the spicy sauce ingredients together and spread a layer onto the base of a brioche bun. Top with lettuce, followed by the cooked chicken burgers, sliced red onion, and the crispy bacon. Serve with homemade wedges (see page 54) and coleslaw.

pasta
Homepride